Bank
Raids

© Haynes Publishing, 2013

The right of Claire Welch to be identified as the author of this Work has been asserted by her in accordance with the Copyright, Designs & Patents Act 1988.

First published in 2013

A catalogue record for this book is available from the British Library

ISBN: 978-0-85733-192-2

Published by Haynes Publishing, Sparkford, Yeovil,
Somerset BA22 7JJ, UK
Tel: 01963 442030 Fax: 01963 440001
Int. tel: +44 1963 442030 Int. fax: +44 1963 440001
E-mail: sales@haynes.co.uk
Website: www.haynes.co.uk

Haynes North America Inc., 861 Lawrence Drive, Newbury Park, California 91320, USA

Images © Mirrorpix

Creative Director: Kevin Gardner
Designed for Haynes by BrainWave

Printed and bound in the US

Bank
Raids

From The Case Files of
 and

Claire Welch

Contents

Introduction

Does crime pay? Well, not according to a survey in 2012 carried out by university economists, who used data held by the British Bankers' Association to estimate that the average haul from a bank raid is roughly £20,000. Raiders can expect to increase that amount if they carry a gun, and also reap more rewards by having a larger gang. However, the chances of being caught will increase significantly with each raid carried out.

Bank raids are fascinating. Who raids banks, and why? What do they do with the money if they escape with the loot, and what happens to the third of raiders who fail in their missions?

Prison taught criminals a great deal about villainy, especially during the mid to latter part of the 20th century. Alliances to successful crime were forged while criminals were inside. Prisons were huge commodity exchanges of "tradecraft", as well as information about where and when crimes were to be committed. This was particularly true after Home Office policy in the 1960s opted to distribute the most desperate criminals throughout regional prisons. The intention was to reduce the possibility of conspiracies behind bars, but the effect was to "seed" the entire system with criminal celebrities, or "faces". Not only did these criminals act as gurus to young hopefuls, they were also in an ideal position to spot and recruit promising newcomers to the "profession".

Improbable as it may seem, some criminals looked back on their stints in prison as the most pleasant times of their lives.

Roger Dennhardt was typical: although a celebrity "face" of the underworld, he was no exception. His story is covered in 1968, but here are some of the memories he had of his time as a mastermind bank raider.

Dennhardt enjoyed his time in Maidstone prison, where he spent 18 months. He had been sent there for what became known as the "Bonnie and Clyde" raids – a series of crimes carried out in 1968 with two other youths and a girl. Still only 20, he studied English, German, maths and navigation (with a view to a possible future in drug smuggling). "I discovered books, discovered I had a brain," he said. He became articulate and widely read, and a logical and informed thinker – qualities later greatly appreciated by his companions when it came to putting a crime together. Dennhardt told police years later that it was while he was in jail that he learnt the art of crime. It was while in Maidstone prison that he met his guru, Fred Sinfield, a seasoned armed robber eight years his elder. Sinfield took the younger man aside, and told him that he had potential. Sinfield said that he was part of the best firm in London, and told Dennhardt that he could earn a great deal of money from his "craft". Dennhardt said: "Armed robbery wasn't that prevalent in 1968. There was one North London firm, two in South London and a couple of East Enders. But the East Enders are not great armed robbers. They're all talk – just want people to know how active they are as criminals. The rest of bent London regard East Enders as no value at all."

Dennhardt went on to form two other significant friendships in

Maidstone. He teamed up with Philip Trusty and John Irish, both armed robbers of a similar age to himself. The three had more to learn from and to teach each other than Dennhardt had been getting from his prison education classes. When they were released, there was not much doubt about what they would do. "When I left prison, I was still in two minds about going straight. But after my first few touches, that was it – because the excitement was too important." From this point on, until around April 1972, he was committed wholeheartedly to the cause. At the age of 21 he was fit, smart, educated, lacking neither guidance nor the love of any number of good women. He could hardly have made a more conscious decision to live outside the law. Prison had decided him on a criminal career, and in no way deterred him whatsoever. It had exactly the opposite effect that it was supposed to. The Home Office initiative, rather than leading to a break-up of criminal activities, had only helped to further the establishment of a huge criminal network.

Dennhardt's newly founded firm steamed around the South of England knocking over – as it was termed in the early 1980s – banks and post offices with cool skill and cunning. The takes ranged from £1,000 to £60,000. At the earliest opportunity, the firm put into practice a theory of Dennhardt's which became a trademark – the rear-entry bank raid. "I'd long since worked out that all the fortifications going up in the banks that were tired of being hit were at the front around the counters. But the rickety old backs and sides were left as they were." The gang planted electronic bugs to let them know when premises like pubs were clear.

Then there was the pressing matter of wheels. One of the major prison crafts was the manufacture of keys, or "fiddlers". Dennhardt had a set that would open most cars; but he preferred to prowl suburban garages looking for vehicles with the keys left inside. "If you use keys, you're setting a pattern. Police can get to the computer and say: 'Well, on this date, and this date, these cars were nicked using proper keys.' You've set up a pattern." An inconspicuous new-model car was essential for crime. Apart from anything else, an old one risked an MOT "stop". The firm worked steadily through the colder part of the year, planning and robbing, planning and robbing. Robbery was a seasonal business. "We used to relax during the summer. We might do a choice pub once a week and get from three to 10 grand. But that's all." Dennhardt continued: "A lot of publicans are fences or minor racketeers of some kind, and they keep piles of cash around." Moving around money, making investments, tracking down and preparing future work took up a lot of the criminals' time. Dennhardt loved pieces of paper; he loved a plan. When asked why he didn't go into business, he replied: "I am in business, I'm an armed robber."

The sawn-off shotgun bucked and roared. Roger Dennhardt's drug-spiked blood froze. For the first time in the eight years he had been robbing at gunpoint he had shot a man. Ironically, it was an accident; something that happened in the confusion of a payroll snatch in North London. But the raid was a turning point in Dennhardt's career as a bandit. He began to be haunted by visions of the security guard in agony. The anxiety and misgivings he came to feel were to lead four years later to his detection. Dennhardt turned his back on crime and became a "supergrass". His information put dozens of crooks in prison. Until his confession, police had no real idea who carried out the £90,000 raid at Murphy's, a firm of building contractors, on 11th March 1976. Murphy's was Dennhardt's most desperate and most successful crime. He had gone prepared to use his gun. This was no different to raids that he carried out on banks.

He told detectives later: "I accepted the role of hit-man the way an Army recruit might accept that one day he would shoot at the enemy." When the moment came, however, Dennhardt found he could not pull the trigger. Until – with adrenaline and amphetamines surging through his veins – came the unscheduled blast from his 12-bore. The assault on Murphy's was a classic example of the thoroughness and tenacity – and courage (although let's not glorify this criminal activity) – with which Dennhardt's firm went about its work. Information is the prime underworld commodity. Dennhardt and his partners were delighted to be put in touch with a former Murphy employee who told them of the huge sum delivered just before 6.00am every Thursday. The five-storey building was put under surveillance from a council enclosure backing onto Highbury Baths, 30yds across the road. The gang included Roger McDowell and Geoff Simms, who crouched in the freezing gloom once a week to watch the Securicor delivery through binoculars. While this particular robbery is not connected to a bank, it does give a fascinating insight into what gangs of criminals did to make sure that their robberies went according to plan.

A VHF radio tuned to police frequency would warn them if they had been spotted, but after the first few weeks they felt part of the scenery, unafraid of the dogs that were led around by Murphy's guards before the van arrived. Only potent greed – a staple of the armed robber – could overcome their despondency at what they saw. Securicor practice, they were well aware, was to put a maximum of £10,000 in a bag. The cash was carried from the van by a pair of guards, through a cordon of burly foremen, to the third-floor accounts department. The prize was estimated to be around £100,000 – far more than most bank raids at this time could offer, when quick snatches might give a few hundred quid. A larger raid might produce a few thousand, but only weekend raids when criminals had time to break the safe uninterrupted gave big takes, and these were often no more than £50,000 at best.

Murphy's was far more interesting for Dennhardt's gang, but the odds were intimidating. Although the firm had recruited two freelancers and had the expertise of Sinfield, there were still only five robbers to a crew of around 15 or so "good guys". Every week that the firm watched and waited disclosed another hazard. How could they get close enough to the building unobserved? Could the escape route be blocked by police or ordinary motorists? Risking a daytime visit to the building on some pretext, several gang members discovered a lift rather than the stairs they had expected. That meant the prize, or a large part of it, could be isolated from them if they took too long to grab it. Finally, a desperate plan was agreed. Dennhardt was to step from behind the fence as the last bags were being carried in and shoot the guard in the leg. McDowell and Sinfield would rush out of hiding from a nearby basement area. They believed that having proved their deadly serious intentions there would be no opposition. Simms, the getaway driver, would blister off with them across Highbury Fields. A four-wheel-drive Range Rover was stolen for the job, together with a back-up car and "change" car. The vehicles were carefully positioned.

McDowell, whose inspiration the raid had been, kept urging Dennhardt to use a .44 Winchester rifle to bring down the guard. No one else objected, but Dennhardt knew that such a shot would probably be fatal. He let the preparations unfold right up to the point where he stepped out of cover and took aim, knowing that he was not going to fire. The raid had to be postponed, and later he told the infuriated others that he had miscalculated – thinking the guard had one more trip to make. He still wanted the prize as much as any of them, though, and he needed to redeem himself.

Using ladders and his considerable scaling skills, Dennhardt found a way into the building through the roof ventilation plant. That changed everything. The following Thursday, Dennhardt skipped down the internal stairs at Murphy's in his Puma trainers just as the first load of money bags arrived at the third floor by lift. He was a deliberately fearsome sight in dark jacket and jeans, face covered by a sweater sleeve drawn into an elastic band, with eyeholes slashed in it. His sawn-off shotgun and the 9mm automatic pistol in his pocket were secured by lanyards around his neck to free his gloved hands so he could grab the bags. Behind, in leather jackets and balaclavas, were Sinfield and McDowell, both with sawn-off shotguns and pistols. Sinfield was the "minder": he was to cover the guards. McDowell was to clear the getaway path. They had all taken amphetamines to heighten their reactions. Dennhardt felt as though he was moving like a piece of well-oiled machinery. His most vital duty was to ensure that a door leading to an alternative exit from the building was not locked. As the lift opened, Dennhardt motioned a terrified guard out with his blunt, authoritative barrel. Glancing towards the glass-panelled exit door, he saw a man duck out of sight on the other side. Had he thrown the lock trapping the gang?

One-handed, Dennhardt fired his sawn-off to blast out the glass. The man reappeared in the door panel just as it shattered. He went down fast. Dennhardt had no time to dwell on what had happened. The air was full of shouts as employees demanded the doors be locked. The robbers bellowed orders, backed up by jabbing gun muzzles. Up the stairs came two men undeterred by Sinfield's evil-looking weapons. When a dog loped towards the gang, Sinfield shot it. The dog howled in an unearthly way, and cried and cried, which was unnerving, but by this time the gang had the bags of money. In a welter of shots Sinfield finished off the dog, and they ran through the shattered door, slipping on the blood of the man Dennhardt had shot as they made their way downstairs. The main door had been locked and several men barred their path, but Sinfield ordered them away. One stayed. "Shoot him!" McDowell ordered. Sinfield raised the shotgun, but Dennhardt shouted: "Leave him!" Instead, the older man blasted through the doors, and they were out.

The Range Rover swung round to meet them, ramming aside a car that one of the foremen was trying to use to block them. They scrambled inside.

To Dennhardt, raids of any description demanded precise techniques. Criminals had to be highly trained. Voices needed to carry authority. "When I went on a robbery," he said, "it's short, sharp commands, no dithering or shilly-shallying." He stated that victims needed to know who was in charge. "The first reaction is fright. Then the victims feel they should make a show of some kind, and you've got to pre-empt that secondary reaction. It must not even arise in their minds." Fear usually came courtesy of the gun and the shock of being raided. Dennhardt explained that the mask wasn't just to hide the raiders' features, but was a way of adding to the victims' fear. It was intended to be frightening, and had to be black to imprint a horrible impression of blackness. Dennhardt said: "A handgun is by far a better weapon in terms of secretion, muzzle velocity, repeating ability, than a sawn-off shotgun, but it doesn't have the visual impact. It's important to have that double-barrelled shotgun. It looks so sinister. You hold it at the midriff and point it up so they can see it. We did a robbery in Bristol once where we had three handguns, and the bloody people never even saw them."

Dennhardt continued: "If you order someone to do something and they don't obey, it doesn't follow you've got to pull the trigger. Other means can bring them to heel." There was, for example, the left hook with the weight of years of fitness training behind it. "I always kept myself in top shape," he said. "If you're not fit and strong you've only got one resort – the trigger." Asked if he would shoot to kill, Dennhardt paused for a long time before he finally replied, "Yes."

After the gang got away from Murphy's, it wasn't long before they were in a nearby "flop" counting their loot. Like many bank raids before, they'd raided the Securicor delivery and the money was exciting, but the leader of the gang saw the robbery as the beginning of the end in terms of his criminal activities. He was shaken by the depth of his own remorse at shooting a man. He was even more shocked by the reaction of his accomplices. Despite the callous readiness to shoot, the two other men were as unnerved as their leader. An important element of criminal mystique had been blown away in the unpredictable barrage. Dennhardt also realized that he would no longer be able to rely on his comrades in arms to give nothing much away. As a notorious criminal and bank raider, he was routinely questioned about the bold and bloody dawn hold-up. Police, however, were none the wiser until four years later, when Dennhardt confessed. His accomplices followed his lead – all except McDowell, who, it had become clear, was a dangerous psychopath. (McDowell spent part of his share of the money on a fast car, which he smashed up – killing himself.)

It was Dennhardt's information that gave police a valuable insight into armed robberies, the rate of which increased during the 1960s. It gave them a look into a previously unknown underworld.

They discovered that what most bandits wanted in a well-organized campaign was a woman who would do what she was told. Most criminals, they found out, had "robber's dogs", the type of women who the robbers could do things with that they wouldn't do with their wives. Depending on the money he made, a bandit would often keep a wife at home and his robber's dog, like his crime car, somewhere else. It was the height of selfishness, but typical of many criminals. Most robber's dogs were described by the criminals who talked about this as "slags at heart", but good looking, shapely and flashy. These women loved robbers. They loved the men described as "faces", but they could also come after their men harder than the "Old Bill". There were two types: those who were highly sexually motivated themselves, and those who used sex to get other things they wanted, like money and status. Many of the women involved with robbers were extremely young and not afraid of "bed-hopping". Women could start as a robber's dog as young as 15, when they were known as "springers". Dennhardt's own young girlfriend got together with him at the age of 15, but she had been sexually active since she was 13 years old. She wasn't the only woman who Dennhardt shared his huge income with. "Most robbers have a high libido. All the ones I know are capable of going with a woman a night." These women were expected to be able to deal with the police as and when necessary. They didn't need to be bright, but they did need to know how to be discreet and to keep their mouth shut.

Melissa told Roger Dennhardt she was 20 when they met in a

disco where promising young West London criminals used to hang out. When he said she looked remarkably mature for her age, she was greatly amused. She had just turned 15 years old. Melissa's parents wanted her to go to France to study, but instead she moved into Dennhardt's flat in Edgware. The couple called themselves the Parkins. The slender brunette hoped she and her handsome lover looked just a little different from their associates. She wasn't impressed with the other women and, unlike them, had no idea what he did for a living when she met Dennhardt. He had told her that he dealt in used cars, and Melissa had accepted this, never questioning it until her man was nicked. Melissa described how the women wanted clothes with initials all over them, perfect dyed blonde hair, and too much make-up for their hard faces. Much of their clothing was stolen from stores like Harrods, Harvey Nichols and Selfridges. The best stuff was saved for when they visited their men in prison. Melissa described going to visit Dennhardt in Brixton prison. She dressed as smartly and as carefully as possible, more to impress the other women than to impress him. Once Melissa realized how much of a "face" Dennhardt was, she found it quite exciting. His status helped to make an impressionable young woman feel important. Melissa stated as fact that some women were turned on by crime. It wasn't the done thing for women to gain comfort, or seek it, from another robber, but it was quite common, once a man was in prison, for his robber's dog to start looking for someone else.

Dennhardt was part of the Harrods fiasco in 1976. Christmas

was on its way, and the Harrods bags were getter fatter and fatter. The estimated haul was £4m. There was an uneasy alliance of firms involved in the planned raid, and Dennhardt had a bad feeling about the job. The target was the Harrods take, delivered by Security Express van from the Knightsbridge store in London to the Midland Bank in Sloane Street. The IRA had been busy and Knightsbridge was teeming with police – many of whom were armed. The area was also full of "black rats", as robbers traditionally called cab drivers. This highly efficient workforce was notorious for trying to impede armed robberies in their city. What worried Dennhardt most, however, was some of the gangs' insistence that they arm themselves with Molotov cocktails to discourage pursuit. He had instincts which had served his firm well, and something felt wrong. On 20th December 1976, the 11 bank raiders went into action regardless.

On his way to the robbery, Dennhardt's tube was late. He changed to another but it was just as slow. He surfaced at Great Portland Street, having travelled from Edgware. It was raining, and only five minutes before the cash delivery might be arriving at the bank. He could not get a taxi to take him to the rendezvous, so he wrenched a bike from its chain and set off desperately to pedal across London. The van he had stolen was already full of milk bottles containing petrol when he arrived, and the robbers were behind schedule. They all sheltered in the van, trying to avoid the guns they were carrying. Sinfield had gained a reputation with guns in confined spaces, and had already injured his friends on a number of occasions.

At last, it was time to go. The assault team swarmed up the rear wall of the bank by ladder. They smashed a window and the alarm began to shriek. Dennhardt leapt across benches and counters to where the Harrods sacks were usually piled. There was nothing: the money was already locked away. He fired into the lock of a cupboard door, where they thought they could get through: they believed that the money had already been sent down the chute to the bank vaults. They did not know that the vault door was open. Cursing madly, they made their way out of the bank and into the waiting van. The cupboard contained the money they were looking for. Their haul would have been £236,600. There was also another £600,000 sitting next to the Harrods bags, and in the accessible vault was a further £4m. "Got there too late and left too early," said a philosophical Dennhardt. His criminal exploits would continue for a time, but not for long.

In prison, or out, the most important thing to a robber, apart from money, is the respect he is given thanks to his success and status. A "face" needs to be recognized. It was expected that a face could mix with other faces and have the attention of admiring women. The pinnacle was to own your own nightclub. Many night-time criminals changed their appearance frequently to throw police off the scent. Faces were liked by almost everybody who moved in their circles, be they burglars or safe-crackers. These criminals had a dignity of their own, according to underworld sources, but they didn't have the same esteem as faces. These men were hard core. They were hard men who talked and thought the same way, and had an instinctive feel for the strategy of a crime. But being a criminal coloured their view of the world. Dennhardt believed that almost everyone a robber encountered was a criminal in some way, or at least dishonest; even the victims. He told police in the early 1980s that during the 1960s and 1970s sums stolen were frequently exaggerated, so that the victim could work an insurance fiddle. People were even known to make false claims for wounds allegedly inflicted during a raid. And, with a great deal of stuff left lying around, it wasn't unusual for a robber to be robbed himself.

Bandits were often tempted to buy the best with their looted fortunes, but there was a danger of overdoing it. It was a mistake to have an ostentatious car: this was a signal to the police that you were up to something. One villain made the mistake of buying a Rolls-Royce, but found he had gone too far when none of his former associates would speak to him any more. Some suggested that a powerful BMW was the answer. The police weren't particularly interested in this middle-class car of the 1970s, but it gave robbers enough power to "boot it" if they needed to evade the law. Automatic transmissions were out because they couldn't take off as quickly. Saab owners were reassured to know that their vehicles were thought to be the most thiefproof, and therefore unlikely to be stolen for a raid. This was down to the complicated door locks they possessed. It was also because the complicated ignition system, located down by the handbrake, required the car to be in reverse gear before the key could be removed, thereby locking the gears rather than the ignition. The ideal car for a bank raid was a very quick four-door and nondescript vehicle. In the early 1980s, Peugeots, BMWs, Granadas and Rovers became the popular cars of choice. It was suggested that motorbikes might even take off as a favoured means of transport.

Over many years in and out of prison, a number of criminal masterminds attempted to understand the complicated laws of evidence. One of the things that bank raiders became good at was "fitting up" the police as soon as possible before a case made it to court. What this meant was that even if the case still went to court the police officer's credibility was in question. This in turn brought into question the evidence brought against the criminal. Bribing jurors and befuddling witnesses were all part of the game.

While new technology has meant that bank raids are no longer the swift, deadly crimes that they once were, the criminal underworld is still full of those who are willing to raise the stakes in order to carry out a daring raid in return for a massive haul.

This book takes a look at a number of famous bank raids from the past 100 years, and discovers the changes that technology has brought about for the modern bank robber, as well as delving into the history of raids. From the earliest documented bank raids, committed at the turn of the 20th century, and the first use of a getaway car in 1911, we take a chronological look at the masterminds behind some of the greatest robberies ever committed.

1906 – Moscow, London and St Petersburg

A huge bank robbery took place on 21st March 1906 in Moscow, when 20 armed men with revolvers entered the Mutual Credit Society Bank, in the centre of the city near the Bourse, just before closing time. The gang covered the banking assistants with their weapons, pillaged the bank and managed to get away with £90,000 in gold and paper. They then made off, with the guards – who had recently been reprimanded about protecting the bank – failing to stop them.

While no one was hurt in the raid, it was a different story in London two months later, in late May, when Archibald Wakley, a promising young painter and member of the Pre-Raphaelite Brotherhood, was found dead at his studio in Monmouth Road, Westbourne Grove. It was meant to be Wakley's year. He had just had a painting entitled *A Sleeping Beauty* accepted by the Academy for their 1906 exhibition, but the 30-year-old, who worked long hours at the studio – even sleeping there on many occasions – was found murdered by the building's caretaker, Mrs Mercer, who stumbled across his body outside his studio door on the second landing. His head was bruised and battered, and he had clearly suffered a violent death. Wakley was wearing trousers and a waistcoat only, and he held a key in his hand. Detectives believed that he had disturbed a gang of bank robbers who had been attempting to enter a branch of the London and County Bank – next door – through a trapdoor on the roof, and they had killed the artist in a desperate effort to escape.

Scotland Yard detectives arrived quickly by car and made a careful examination of the murder scene, though the perpetrators had obviously long gone: it was presumed that their capture would be extremely difficult. Using magnesium light, the detectives had the room and surroundings photographed. It was rumoured that the gang could be the one that had been responsible for a bank raid in St James' Street the week before. In Monmouth Road it appeared that they had intended to make their way from the trapdoor to the cellar, before breaking through the vaults of the bank. Detectives believed that Wakley had been woken by suspicious noises and had gone to investigate, only to meet a violent death. The bank's porter slept over the premises, on the same floor as Wakley's studio. Only a thick wall separated the men, but the porter had heard nothing. A well-known artist named Chevalier, who worked on the floor below where Wakley was found, said: "The murder was a brutal one, the head being terribly battered. The body was found wrapped in the bedclothes; this must have been done by those who committed the crime." The unfortunate artist had dined at Simpson's the night before the attack, and his distressed father identified the body before it was removed to Paddington Green mortuary.

There were no more bank raids that made the newspapers in London that year, but in December, Odessa in Russia was under attack when 12 men raided the St Petersburg International Commerce Bank on Wednesday 13th. The 12 men held revolvers over bank staff as they stole £2,900 in cash and £6,200 in securities. Eleven of the men succeeded in escaping, but one gang member was on the point of capture when he killed a police officer, and then turned his gun on himself.

1908 – Reminiscences of the Wild West, Butch Cassidy and the Sundance Kid

In Tulsa, Oklahoma, three robbers broke open the safe of the bank at Fairland on 5th June 1908, and escaped on horseback with £2,000.

This was also the year that Butch Cassidy and the Sundance Kid were supposed to have died – killed by the rifles of 100 soldiers in Bolivia. But were they? Not according to Lula Parker-Betenson. The youngest sister of Butch Cassidy claimed many years later that: "They died with their boots off, in bed, back home in the United States." The newspapers worked themselves up into a flurry over Lula's claims, which dispelled the Western legend about two of the most notorious robbers of the early 20th century. For 45 years she kept quiet, but eventually she told the story of how her brother was even more fascinating than Hollywood could ever make him. He was a sort of six-gun Robin Hood, who robbed the rich to pay the poor and never killed a man, though he was one of the fastest and most accurate guns in the West. Only one sheriff ever tried to find Robbers' Roost, the hideout of the gang known as the Wild Bunch. But the outlaws found him first. They took his horse, stripped him of his boots and trousers and pointed him in the direction of the nearest town. From a thousand vantage points it was possible to pick off unwanted visitors approaching Robbers' Roost, and to Butch Cassidy it would have been child's play. He didn't shoot, and the lawman went home footsore but alive.

From stories such as this the legend of Butch Cassidy grew, and cowhands and miners took him to their hearts. Butch Cassidy was born Robert Leroy Parker in the hamlet of Beaver, Utah in 1866. His father, who came from Accrington, Lancashire, had crossed the sprawling plains of the United States pulling a handcart, on one of the great Mormon treks west. Butch was the oldest of 13 children; Lula was the youngest. They lived in a log cabin in the tiny town of Circleville. Lula said: "I was only six months old when Butch rode away. He was 18." The free ranges of Utah, Wyoming and Colorado were teeming with stray cattle, which famers were rounding up and stamping with their own brands. It was only a small step from that to straightforward rustling. Young Robert Leroy Parker was quick to learn. He left home to work in the mines of Colorado, and fell in with an outlaw called Mike Cassidy. When Mike had to leave the area in a hurry, with the law hot on his heels, young Parker adopted his surname and called himself George Cassidy – nobody knew where he got the name George. The law caught up with Cassidy only once during his entire rampage through the West. In 1894, he was caught stealing horses in Wyoming and jailed for two years. He gave his age as 27. He became Butch Cassidy some years later, while working at a butcher's shop in Rock Springs, Wyoming. Lula said: "My brother was never afraid of honest labour. Between bank hold-ups and robbing trains he worked at a multitude of jobs from ranch foreman to miner. Every rancher who employed him said he was the best top hand they ever had.

"All the people liked him, even the law officers. He only robbed banks and railroads and mines, and they weren't popular with the people anyway. He never robbed ordinary people and, in fact, he gave a lot of his loot away. Anyone on hard times could go to him for help. If he didn't have the cash, he'd go out and get it from folks he reckoned had too much anyway. He used to buy supplies and ammunition from a widow who had a store and little farm in Hanksville on the Dirty Devil River.

"The old lady invited him to stay for supper one evening, and while they ate she told him a man was coming that night to foreclose on her farm because she couldn't raise the mortgage money. Butch asked how much was needed. He pulled a roll of bills out of his pocket and gave them to the woman, telling her to hand it over to the man. Butch left, and later that night the mortgage holder came and collected his money and rode away into the darkness. He had only gone about a mile when he was held up and robbed ... but the mortgage deed was already marked 'paid'."

Butch often escaped capture because lawmen had a soft spot for his generous ways. "One Christmas he almost froze to death in a blizzard in the high country of Wyoming. He was rescued by a poor rancher who took him home. When Butch recovered, he rode into town and bought clothes and food and toys for the rancher's kids. But when he returned to the ranch, a sheriff and two deputies were waiting for him. They saw his arms full of toys for the children, and were so impressed that the sheriff told him, 'If you see Cassidy, tell him we're looking for him.' They then rode away."

The Sundance Kid's real name was Harry Longabaugh. He was nicknamed Sundance after serving an 18-month stretch at Sundance, Wyoming for stealing horses. Butch and his gang got away with $32,000 from a Nevada bank in 1900 and headed for Texas. In the border town of San Antonio they bought "dude" clothes, went to a photographer's and posed for a formal group picture. They sent one print to the owner of the bank they had robbed. The picture was picked up by a Pinkerton detective agency man, and the gang had to split up. Butch, Sundance and Etta Place, a schoolteacher from Denver, Colorado, decided to go to South America. "Etta had a real liking for Butch, even though she was Sundance's girlfriend," said Lula. "They went to South America to retire, really. They bought cattle and started ranching down there, but the law came after them, and the bank robberies began all over again."

In 1909, seven years after Butch and Sundance left the United States, the Bolivian Army triumphantly announced that they had killed the pair after they had robbed a silver mine. The grieving family heard the news and thought it was the end of Butch. But 16 years later, a Model T Ford arrived at the family ranch. "A stocky man in city clothes got out," said Lula. "When he grinned, we knew – Butch was back."

He told them the two killed by the Bolivian Army were a pair of greenhorns. At the time, Butch was in an Indian hut miles away recovering from a scorpion bite; Sundance was away on business. "Butch told us that for the first time in his life he felt a free man. The law thought he was dead and he was happy to leave it that way. He told us not to tell anyone that he was still alive, and we never did. He said that Sundance and Etta were back in the United States too. Then, one day, Butch told us he was restless and had to ride on. He wrote to us from time to time, but I never saw him again."

Butch Cassidy spent the rest of his life as a trapper and prospector in Alaska, Wyoming and Washington State. He died in Spokane, Washington, in 1937. He had spent three days with the Sundance Kid that spring, then they separated forever. Sundance died in 1957 and was buried in Casper, Wyoming under the name of Harry Long. Lula wasn't prepared to say where her brother was buried. She was keeping that news to herself until her book about him was published.

1919 – James Shakespear

"Come on, hands up!" read a headline in the *Mirror* on 25th June 1919, when James Herbert Shakespear was committed for trial at Dartford on charges of wounding Robert Leslie. He was charged with wounding the manager of the Belvedere branch of Lloyds Bank, and attempting to murder PCs Darke and Moore. Leslie said that while he was bending over the counter of the bank Shakespear entered, carrying a parcel, and shouted: "Come on, hands up!" He had a revolver in his left hand. PC Darke described how he chased Shakespear in Lime Wood. Shakespear then pointed the revolver at him several times, and eventually fired it. The bullet went through PC Darke's helmet. The case continued ...

1921 – Lloyds Bank, Beccles, and a Robbery in London

Two men armed with revolvers entered Lloyds Bank at Beccles, near Lowestoft, Suffolk, on 1st February 1921, and got away with more than £100 in notes and silver. Inspector Norman of Beccles scoured the district in a motorcycle and sidecar, and close to Mutford he came across the two men. When challenged, they fired 12 shots from their guns and made off. Though he was badly wounded in the knee, the inspector chased the men across ploughed fields and arrested them. They gave addresses in Leyton, and were charged.

Newspapers reported that at 1.20pm on 1st February, two well-dressed young men entered Lloyds Bank and demanded money at gunpoint. The bank manager was at lunch, and an assistant cashier and a junior clerk were threatened. There was nothing they could do to stop the men, who seized several bundles of Treasury notes in the till, some packets of silver and a quantity of loose coins. They left the bank walking backwards and still covering the assistants with their weapons. On the doorstep, they put the guns in their pockets and walked away; one went in one direction, one in another. The police were quickly on the scene. Inspector Norman, who was in charge of the investigation, borrowed a Swift motorcycle from Huntley Durrant, a local auctioneer, who drove the vehicle while Norman took to the sidecar. After scouring the countryside for 5 miles around Beccles, the police inspector and the auctioneer came across two men leaving the main road for a by-road. The inspector left the sidecar and told the men he wanted to have a word with them. They whipped out their guns and fired six bullets each, then made off after throwing their revolvers away. Inspector Norman chased the men across the fields, and came to a gate where he saw a farmer. The farmer lent him a gun, and the inspector was joined by several locals. The two fugitives were gradually hemmed in. Pointing the farmer's gun at the two men, the inspector told the two men to put their hands up. Then he asked them to take off their coats, and he arrested them. He had been chasing the men for 10 minutes before he noticed that he had a gunshot wound to his right knee; another bullet had grazed his leg. Subsequently, the inspector found a number of banknotes which had been set on fire behind a hedge, and a quantity of silver coins. The two arrested men were taken to Beccles police station and were brought before the police court on 3rd February 1919. Inspector Norman was taken to hospital and given an X-ray. Durrant praised the inspector for his courage and determination.

Arthur James Parsley, 18, and Frank Jarvis, 19, both from Leyton, were remanded at Beccles, charged with the theft of £150 from Lloyds Bank. Henry James Hughes said the prisoners entered the bank and pulled guns on him and the junior clerk. They demanded all the cash that had been in the till. Hughes described to the court how he handed over the money, but that he had done so slowly in order to gain time. He was told by Parsley and Jarvis that if he didn't meet their demands or if he raised the alarm he would be shot. Parsley, however, denied using threats. Superintendent Cowper said that Inspector Norman, owing to his injuries, would be unable to attend court for a fortnight, and the men were remanded until then. The men's guns were found – loaded – by police in a field close to where they were arrested.

That same year, in August, Howard Power, aged 16, was charged in the South-Western Court of stealing £100 from the Streatham Hill branch of the London County, Westminster and Parrs Bank. The young clerk, from Hackney, was remanded when bail was refused. The criminal offered no defence. He had entered the bank and asked for an application form for 5½ per cent Treasury Bonds. He grabbed a bundle of £1 Treasury notes from the counter, and then disappeared. However, he was later detained at Commercial Street police station. It turned out that Power had stolen the money because some other teenagers were blackmailing him.

1922 – Trouble in the North

Two detectives made a surprise arrest on 25th January 1922 at a village on the Firth of Forth near Edinburgh, in connection with the alleged misappropriation of Canadian Grand Trunk Pacific bonds with a value of £20,000. The detectives from Edinburgh were making inquiries at the fishing village of Newhaven, in connection with a recent bank hold-up at Granton, when they met a young man in the area who, they thought, answered a description circulated by Pinkerton's Detective Agency of a clerk with a firm in Ontario, Canada, who was believed to have landed in England in October 1921. The detectives questioned the man, then arrested him. He was taken to London. William Stewart was eventually sentenced in March 1922 to eight years by the High Court in Edinburgh in connection with the Granton bank robbery.

In July 1922, three men were due to be brought before Manchester magistrates charged with participation in a sensational robbery earlier in the month at the Manchester and Liverpool District Bank, Prestwich. On 29th November 1922 sentences of 10 years penal servitude were passed at Manchester Assizes on Bartley Iago, a 26-year-old collier, and John Foley, a 23-year-old labourer, for holding up the Prestwich bank and shooting their pursuers. The men had thought they would get away in a taxi with £245.

1925 – Swindon Under Siege

James Walsh was alleged to have stolen a car from Harley Street, which was later used at a bank raid in Swindon alongside bank robber John O'Sullivan. He then tried to shoot Divisional Inspector Ward when he was arrested at a boarding house in Waterloo Road. The dramatic story of the arrests came on 31st May 1925, when the Tower Bridge police court was told that the two Irishmen, Walsh and O'Sullivan, were charged with stealing the car, raiding the bank and threatening Ward with a loaded revolver. The revolver just clicked and didn't fire when Walsh tried to shoot the inspector. Luckily for Ward, it was faulty.

1926 – Daring Raids in Portsmouth, Leicester and Liverpool

Twenty-four-year-old John Thurston, an ex-soldier, appeared at Portsmouth police court on 30th March 1926, charged with robbing William F Mountford of £50 – the property of Lloyds Bank – and of shooting at him with intent to murder. It was alleged that while running from the bank Thurston also fired at two other people. He was eventually overpowered by Sgt Hopkinson, who jumped on the accused as he tried to flee the scene.

Two months later a man armed with a dummy revolver carried out a daring bank robbery in Leicester. The cashier, Mr Chapman, was alone in the Braunstone Gate branch of Barclays Bank when he was approached by a man. The visitor suddenly pulled the realistic dummy weapon on him. Mr Chapman told the *Daily Mirror* that he had just finished his lunch when the man came into the bank, covered him with the gun, and said: "Hand over the lot, and be quick about it. Get on with it." The weapon was pointed at Mr Chapman all the time, and the man forced him against a drawer containing the cash, seizing notes on the counter to the value of £250. As soon as the man was outside, the cashier gave chase, shouting: "Stop, thief." A number of men were passing, but failed to realize what was happening. A girl tackled the man, however, and nearly brought him to the ground. He succeeded in throwing her off, although she clung to him pluckily for some time. Then he rode off on a bicycle. Another cyclist gave chase, and after a time was able to pull up ahead of the fugitive. He threw his bike in front of the bank robber and brought him to the ground. All the money was recovered and the man was arrested.

In October 1926, four men were shot at and wounded by a thief who raided a branch of the District Bank in Liverpool's Haymarket. He fled through the streets, firing at his pursuers as he went. All the wounded were in a serious condition. Statements were given by, among others, the bank cashier, who was shot as he called for help, a policeman and two men who joined in the chase. Three of the men were shot down as they pursued the robber through the streets around the raided bank. The chase only ended when a motorist blocked a narrow street with his car and enabled a policeman to bring the man down with his truncheon. Only £5 had been stolen from the bank. The arrested man appeared in court on 14th October 1926.

Mr William Tooly, the bank cashier, was counting silver when the bank raider entered. The man whipped out a revolver and shouted: "Hand over!" But Mr Tooly bravely drew the money towards himself and shouted for help. As he did so, the man shot him in the stomach, seized a bag of silver and bolted, shooting into the crowd that chased him. The other men injured were John Stevenson, Robert Vipond and PC Harold Clark. All were described as in a serious condition – and John Stevenson had to have an operation to have a bullet removed from his skull. The arrested man was William McAllister, a Liverpool man, who had recently returned to his home town from the south of Ireland. It was stated that an empty six-chamber revolver was found in his possession. William Calkeld, the manager of the bank, was the first to give chase.

"I was sitting in my private room with a friend when I heard Mr Tooly call out," he said. "There was a shot, and I rushed into the general office in time to see him fall to the ground. The raider still had the revolver in his hand, and he bolted through the front door. I followed, and he raced across the North Haymarket. Passers-by, attracted by shouts of 'Stop, thief', joined in the chase, and the thief finding that he was being cornered, turned and whipped out his revolver, driving us back. In North Street, a civilian flung himself at the man and tried to bring him to the ground. Then there was a muffled shot and the civilian collapsed. An elderly man and I were now nearest, and just as we were about to seize the raider he turned round and fired again. I escaped, but the man beside me fell."

A policeman now joined in the pursuit along with workmen who were at the corner of the street. Again, the man fired, but this time the bullet only shattered the glass of a window. Then he made away down Juvenal Street, followed most closely by a policeman. When he arrived at the corner of Grosvenor Street, the raider stopped, took careful aim at the oncoming officer and fired. The constable fell to the ground, calling out: "Oh, I am hit." Mr J Hartley, a barman at the Haymarket Hotel, gave a graphic description of the chase. "The man was running down Great Homer Street," he said, "brandishing his revolver and occasionally glancing round at his pursuers, who were rapidly gaining on him. At the corner of North Haymarket, a man challenged him. He gave chase for a few yards and was then shot down. The crowd continued to gain, and I was about 10 yards from the thief when he fired at Police Constable Clark.

"When he reached Grosvenor Street, a man with a motor-car ran across his path and stopped him. At the same moment a constable dashed up and felled him with his truncheon." Another eyewitness of the chase stated that he heard shots and saw a man followed by a big crowd. PC Clark was on point duty, and he dashed at the man, throwing off his cape and drawing his truncheon as he ran. Two shots were fired in quick succession, and the policeman fell. PC Smethick, of the Market force, who made the arrest, became famous as the leader of the Liverpool police strike, and was later dismissed from the force. The arrested man was brought before magistrates on 15th October. Following the raid and shootings, William McAllister, aged 20, was remanded in custody.

McAllister was charged with shooting four men with intent to do grievous bodily harm. He was further charged with assaulting Tooly and stealing £2 8s, which was the property of the bank. Howard Roberts, prosecuting, said the accused entered the Liverpool District Bank in Great Homer Street where 20-year-old William Tooly was the only member of staff present. McAllister levelled a revolver at him and shouted for the cashier to raise his hands. Tooly picked up a paperweight, which he threw at McAllister, at the same time shouting to the manager of the bank who was in a room at the rear. McAllister fired, and the bullet entered Tooly's chest. While McAllister was running away – chased by the bank manager and several civilians – he shot at his pursers; but he said in court that he hadn't been aiming at anyone specific. Police evidence given at the time stated that McAllister said of PC Clark: "Well, he got in the way of the gun," and in reply to the charge of shooting at Stevenson: "I did not aim at him." McAllister was found to have in his possession £2 4s in silver. He said that he wished to make a statement, but on hearing that anything he said could be used in evidence he changed his mind, but said he would answer any questions. Meanwhile, Stevenson remained in a critical condition.

1927 – The Rise of the Getaway Car

London was combed by detectives on 19th October 1927 for a number of men who used a getaway car after robbing a clerk of £85. The clerk, Mr J Southgate, employed by the London Co-operative Society's laundry, was passing along Union Road, Leytonstone, when the attack took place. His bag, which contained silver, was snatched from him, and the men drove off. Hundreds of pounds in notes in the victim's pockets were untouched.

Southgate was being accompanied by Herbert Westall from Ilford at the time. Because of the lightning speed of the hold-up, he was unable to do anything to help. Fifty-four-year-old Southgate was not seriously hurt, and was able to go home after giving a statement to police. "The two men," said an official of the London Co-operative Society, "were taking money to a bank in the High Street in a stout attaché case containing £85 in silver. This the men got away with, but in Southgate's pocket were ... notes.

"The men made no attempt to take this. Southgate and Westall were walking towards the High Street when a blue grey 7cwt Ford car passed them. It stopped, two men sprang out, one of them hit Southgate over the head and sent him staggering against a wall, while the other snatched his bag. Both men made off before Westall could move a hand. It was all over in about a quarter of a minute. Southgate was not seriously hurt, and I should say he was struck a violent blow with a man's fist."

The theft must have been timed to the second for the men to catch Southgate and Westall at the spot where they were least liable to be seen. Several people, however, witnessed the hold-up but were too startled to take any action. Mrs Coleman, who lived nearby, stated that she heard cries and saw one man was leaning against the wall. "I thought he had been knocked down by the car," she continued. "Suddenly two men dashed towards the waiting car, got in and were round the corner in a flash. Another man ran after the car, shouting. His friend, as I now know him to be, leaned feebly up against the wall, crying: 'Stop them, stop them, they have robbed me.'" Both the assailants were young and between 25 and 30 years of age. One was wearing a blue suit and the other a very dark grey coat and a grey cap of a lighter shade. The police released a more detailed description of the men following the hold-up.

1928 – Wild Chase
in Germany

Heidger, the bandit for whom the police of Cologne had been searching for some time, was captured on 26th October 1928 at the house where he was hiding out. He was discovered by a woman servant in a cellar of a villa that belonged to Herr Oertel, a director of the Colonia Insurance Company. He immediately fired his gun at the woman, but he missed, and she ran away and raised the alarm. Herr Oertel locked himself with his two children in a bedroom and tried to telephone the police, but Heidger had cut the wires. The armed police and the fire brigade arrived almost immediately. The police advanced under cover of bulletproof shields, and broke open the doors of the villa before throwing hand grenades into the room where the man was hiding. The criminal then shot and wounded a police officer.

After more hand grenades had been thrown, the firing from the room stopped, and Heidger was found sitting in a corner with five bullet wounds in his legs, two in the chest and one in the shoulder. He put up his hands and called out: "I have enough. I surrender." His injuries were found not to be serious at a nearby hospital. Heidger and his brother had been involved in an all-night chase a few days before, being wanted in connection with a bank hold-up in München Gladbach. They were spotted by the police in Cologne.

A wild chase followed, in which 400 police joined, but although Heidger was seen to jump over a wall into a large garden he could not be found. At one point in the chase, the two fugitives held up a tram at gunpoint, cleared it of passengers, then drove it at a breakneck speed to the banks of the Rhine. When they abandoned it, Heidger's brother was shot dead.

1929 – A Surprisingly Fake Hold-up

On 31st May 1929, a widespread search was made by the Glossop, Derbyshire, police for the assailant of Arnold B Whiteley, assistant manager of the Henry Street branch of Lloyds Bank. The ringing of the burglar alarm attracted a constable to the bank about 1.00pm, and he found Mr Whiteley lying on the floor, bound, gagged and under the influence of chloroform. The manager of the bank, Mr R S Ashton, and other members of staff were at lunch at the time. When they returned, it was to discover that £2,718 was missing. A considerable part of the money was in banknotes, and the police were given the numbers on the notes. Whiteley believed that two men took part in the bank raid, and that a car was used. He gave a detailed description of one of the men to police: "Aged about 40, height 5ft. 9in., fairly round face, fresh complexion, small moustache, wearing light raincoat, soft trilby hat and light smoked glasses." A surprising feature was that the bank was next to a Liberal club, which was the centre of a great deal of activity at the time of the raid.

On 3rd June, Whiteley and Henry Farrar, managing director of a firm of cotton doublers from Yorkshire, were jointly charged with the theft of the money. The chief constable of Glossop said he apprehended Farrar at his residence at Bridghouse and brought him to Glossop police station, where he was detained. After being cautioned, he made a statement. Whiteley walked into the police station that same morning and was apprehended. He was also cautioned and made a statement, wanting it noted that he gave himself up voluntarily. The chief constable agreed to this. The bank manager, Mr Ashton, said that he checked the money in Whiteley's possession before the raid. After the raid, he checked again, and the £2,718 was missing. The cashier was solely responsible for the money in his charge. The accused were remanded in custody.

The amazing evidence for the fake hold-up was heard in court in Glossop. The former cashier, Arnold Whiteley, and Henry Farrar were charged with stealing and receiving the money. Mr Lea, prosecuting, said that Whiteley had previously made a statement to the police alleging personal violence on himself and robbery. It appeared that the accused men had been dealing in cotton futures, and it was suggested that Whiteley owed money to Farrar in connection with his deals. Farrar apparently purchased the chloroform and also the cotton wad found over Whiteley's mouth. Whiteley, for his part, arranged a convenient time for the "raid". Farrar attended the bank to bind Whiteley, then left the bank with the bundle of notes, which his accomplice had given him.

The story Whiteley had given did not match with events, and the room where the "hold-up" took place was not disturbed in any way; even Whiteley's clothing was in place. Given this, the chief constable was suspicious and made appropriate inquiries. Mr Bastide, acting for Whiteley, asked that the case might be dealt with summarily. It was the work of amateurs who repented of their act immediately afterwards and gave information to the police. A constable said that there had been no alarm bell, and he had found Whiteley with his feet and hands tied with string and with a cotton wad over his mouth. Artificial respiration was then applied, and when he came around, Whiteley was reported to have said: "Smoked glasses." The chief constable stated that the former cashier said a man came into the bank wearing smoked glasses, and that he thought the man (Farrar) was blind; so he went towards him and asked how he could help. He said that he had been taken by the collar and got a blow to his stomach from the man's knee, which winded him. "I fell on my knees and face, and he fell on my back and put some material in my mouth. My hands were tied behind my back, and when I struggled to get up I felt myself going, and a peculiar taste in my mouth. I realized I was losing consciousness and tried to ring the alarm bell. I knew nothing more until I heard the constable speaking."

After his arrest, Whiteley said he conceived the idea of a bank raid, and Farrar agreed to help. He let Farrar in and was gagged by him. He found himself being overcome, but was fully conscious of thinking about the futility of the whole thing and of struggling to the alarm bell. The accused were committed to Derby Quarter Sessions, while bail of £600 cash was allowed.

1930 – Gang Operating in Warwickshire and Sussex

Breconshire police detained two men and a woman at Hay-on-Wye in connection with an "extraordinary" incident which was said to have occurred at the Midland Bank at Pershore, Worcestershire. The police also took possession of a car and a considerable amount of money. An attractive woman had entered the bank and struck up a conversation with a bank official. Afterwards, she drove away in a car with a man. Later, a sum of money was discovered to be missing from the bank, and following inquiries, a description of the people involved was circulated. The couple were believed to have been connected with a bank robbery at Crawley, Sussex, some time previously, when £70 was stolen.

1932 – American Bank Raiders Make their Mark in Britain

A report in May 1932 highlighted how banks and trust companies in the United States had suffered 288 daylight hold-ups and 37 night burglaries during the six months from September 1931 to the end of February 1932. The figures were given by the manager of the protective department of the American Bankers' Association, and published in the *New York Sun*. The number of hold-ups amounted to two attacks each business day.

"It is gratifying to report that the amount of losses by member banks through robbery ... shows a drop of more than 50 per cent compared with the previous year," the report stated. "During the first half of the association's current fiscal year robbery losses of member banks totaled $715,000 (£143,000), at par, as compared with loot amounting to $1,436,000 (£297,200 at par) taken a year ago. In addition to those material losses of money and securities, one bank employee and four arresting officers were killed." Since the previous August, bank robberies had also cost the lives of 20 criminals, the report concluded.

Gunmen from the United States, it seemed, were beginning to make their mark in Britain as well. In June 1932, an American gunman was sentenced to seven years penal servitude at Exeter Assizes. Richard Philip Elson, 28, was believed to have planned –

along with another two men – to hold up one-man banks throughout the British Isles. Elson and Sidney William Miller, 56, alongside 22-year-old Robert Benjamin McKay, were charged with stealing a car, assaulting a police constable and possessing an automatic pistol with intent to endanger life. Sir Percival Clarke, prosecuting, said that early on 13th April 1932, PC Martin saw the men with a car at Bovisand, near Plymouth. Being suspicious, he got into the car and told them to drive to Plymouth, but he was threatened with a pistol and ordered to get out of the car. DI Lynch, of Scotland Yard, said that when he arrested Elson in bed in a London County Council lodging house, he found the loaded automatic weapon under the man's pillow. Elson and McKay, the inspector added, had been associated with well-known safe-breakers, one of whom, known as The Red, was now in custody. Cross-examined by Elson, Miller agreed that his wife was within 200 or 300yds when the police officer was held up. Elson said: "Why didn't you go to her?" Miller replied: "Because you threatened me. Both you and McKay had revolvers, and the policeman and I were unarmed and I am a cripple." Mr Justice Charles, summing up, referred to the LCC lodging house in which Elson was arrested and said: "Evidence has been given that very undesirable people sleep there. I think it is a matter into which the LCC would be well advised to inquire." Elson was sentenced to seven years, McKay to five years and Miller to three years in jail.

Two more men were arrested in London on 2nd May 1932 in connection with another raid, this time a hold-up in Portsmouth, where the haul was a staggering £23,700. The men appeared before magistrates on 3rd May. The money was stolen the week before from William Snook, a member of staff from Lloyds Bank in Commercial Road, Portsmouth, whose bag was snatched from him by some men in a convertible. Mr Poor, the bank porter, who was accompanying Francis Neville "William" Snook, jumped on the running-board of the car and was injured in the affray.

The prisoners were Alfred George Hinds, 43, from Camberwell and John Parker, 48, from Tarn Street on the New Kent Road, south-east London. They were accused jointly with two other men – not in custody – of assaulting Robert George Poor and William Snook, and robbing them of money belonging to Lloyds Bank Limited. DI Turner, head of the Criminal Investigation Department at Portsmouth, said that on Sunday he went to Tarn Street with Inspector Brooks, of the Flying Squad, and there saw Parker. He was taken to Cannon Row police station, and on Monday, a search was made by the Flying Squad for Hinds, who was later arrested in Newington Causeway, and also taken to Cannon Row. A number of witnesses from Portsmouth had been sent to London, and an identification parade was held. The inspector added that the first witness to be called, a lorry driver named Boyes, of Portsea, picked out Parker. A second witness, Charles Pittman, a corporation bus driver, picked out Hinds. A third witness, Miss Higgins, also picked out Parker. On the evidence, the inspector asked for a remand, saying that the condition of Poor was still critical.

Parker applied for leave to send a telegram to his wife, notifying her that he had been remanded to Winchester. The Bench agreed, and ordered the two men to be remanded in custody for a week. Usually prisoners were taken from Portsmouth to Winchester in a prison van, and hundreds of people assembled outside the Guildhall to see their departure. The crowd were disappointed in this case, though, as the police brought the men out by another door and quietly walked them over to the railway station, from where they were taken by train to Winchester.

The sequel to the men's court appearance came at Winchester Assizes on 8th June 1932, when Parker and Hinds, alongside Benjamin Bennett, 30, were charged with robbing the two Lloyds Bank employees and using violence. Mr O'Connor, for the prosecution, said that a very disquieting feature of the case was that nothing had been recovered. The men had got away with every penny. The Crown undertook to prove that the man who struck down the bank messenger was Parker, and that Bennett drove the car, while Hinds was at least in the car.

On 11th July, two judges tried cases in which the bandits were found guilty, and in each case ordered the cat (cat-o-nine-tails whip) in addition to prison sentences. Mr Justice Avory, sitting at Winchester, said that the time had come when stern measures must be taken to repress this class of offence. The trial was continued before him of charges of robbery with violence of a sum of £23,977 at Portsmouth. He heard that as a Treasury official and a messenger were carrying the money in the street, four men drove up alongside them, and one of them jumped out and struck the messenger on the head with a blunt instrument. He seized the money and jumped back into the car, which drove away at speed.

Evidence was given that Hinds had started lodging in Portsmouth a few streets away from Lloyds Bank. It was said that he had a bag with him which he never let out of his sight. Bennett – a mechanic – was said to have found employment at a garage near the town (the car used in the robbery was found there). Four men's caps were discovered in the car. The prisoners produced evidence of alibis, and tried to prove that they were unknown to each other and were in London on the day of the robbery. Parker was given five years, Hinds four years and Bennett three years, and each was to be given 15 strokes of the cat.

At the same time that these men were sentenced, four young men who took part in the hold-up of a cashier and secretary at Stratford were ordered to receive a whipping in addition to imprisonment at the Old Bailey. Charles Boss got three years and 12 strokes of the cat, Patrick Moore received 12 months and 18 strokes with the birch, while Harry Bond received the same sentence, including the birch. Frederick Stewart was sentenced to nine months imprisonment for receiving only. The two men who were attacked, Arthur Holmes and James Fisher, had £120 in wages stolen from them. Around £20 of this had been in an attaché case that Holmes was carrying. Fisher had received a violent blow which fractured his jaw, while Holmes was struck on the face and arms, causing him to drop the case.

In August 1932, counsel for the defence in the case against

Parker and Hinds was sharply rebuked by Mr Justice Swift in the Court of Criminal Appeal for a remark described as "an impertinence". The two men had both appealed against their sentences to Justices Swift, Humphreys and Goddard. Wickham, acting for Parker, criticized the summing up of Justice Avory with regard to an alibi put forward by his client. Both appeals were dismissed.

In December that same year, two men and a woman were detained in the Ardwick district of Manchester in connection with an armed raid on Williams Deacons branch bank at Third Avenue, Trafford Park, Manchester, when the manager and assistant manager were injured and about £900 was taken. The three accused were to appear at the county police court in the city on 12th December. The two men were from Glasgow and the woman from Nelson in Lancashire. All three were living in the Manchester area at the time of the hold-up. The charges were heard a week later when James Reynolds, 25, Patrick Hickey, 22, and Lillian Torkington, 18, were further remanded in custody. Reynolds and Hickey were charged with stealing £903 from the bank and with assaulting two clerks. Torkington was charged with receiving the money, knowing it was stolen. It was stated that police keeping watch outside a Manchester hotel saw Torkington arrive in a car. She went into the hotel, and when she left with Reynolds she was arrested alongside him. Around £800 and a revolver were found inside the young woman's suitcase.

The two bank clerks who were struck on the head with the butt-end of the revolver, by the two men accused of raiding the bank and stealing the money, were in court to give evidence in January 1933. Walter Butterworth, a clerk with Williams Deacons Bank Ltd, said that he had been prodded with the revolver and forced to kneel down. He was also forced to have his hands tied while the gun was pointing at his chest. The second clerk, Frederick Eadesforth from Pendleton, said that when the men could not open the safe he was ordered to open it for them. Because the men were so threatening, he obeyed. He was also ordered to open the coffers in the safe. The revolver was pressed into his side during the whole of this ordeal.

On 3rd January 1933, in the same case, a man collapsed in the witness box and had to be revived with water. The man was so frightened when giving evidence against the accused because he had had a conversation with the accused, in which they had admitted to the robbery. First in the witness box, though, was Leonard Walker, who went to the house where Hickey and Reynolds were lodging two days after the raid to play cards with them. During the game, another man named Quinless mentioned the robbery, at which point the two accused agreed that it was they who had carried it out. Alexander Quinless was also called into court to give evidence, and after admitting that he knew Reynolds and Hickey had carried out the raid he partially collapsed in the witness box. Quinless was obviously frightened, and the chairman in court urged him to collect himself. When he was able to resume as a witness, Quinless claimed that he had been unable to go to the police because he was frightened, and did not want to get "dragged" into the affair.

1933 – The Duffy Brothers

Two brothers, described as "dangerous men", who six years earlier had been sentenced to 20 years imprisonment in Sing Sing for an armed bank robbery, and had been subsequently pardoned, were in Newcastle on 28th June 1933, where they were sentenced to 10 years. They were also sentenced to receive 15 strokes of the cat for a similar hold-up. Joseph Duffy, 30, and Thomas Duffy, 28, from Edinburgh, were found guilty of carrying out a raid, of which the judge, Mr Justice Charles said: "thank goodness, is practically unknown in this country". He added: "When it is carried out it must and shall be suppressed with an iron hand."

Police told the court that after being pardoned, the Duffys were deported from the United States. When they returned to Britain, Thomas Duffy published his life story under the title *My Life as an American Gangster*. In it, he described the bank robbery the brothers carried out in the USA. The methods they employed were identical to those they then used in a bank raid in Newcastle. They were charged with this crime alongside William Myles Abbot, 32, who was also from Edinburgh. Found guilty and described by the judge as a "catspaw," Abbot received 12 months imprisonment in the second division.

Just before the bank closed, customers told the court how three men entered with their hats pulled well down. They were wearing masks and carrying revolvers. They shouted: "Stand still, everybody, and put your hands up." Among those forced to line up against a wall at gunpoint was a 15-year-old girl. Since the robbery, the girl had suffered such mental distress that she was unable to come to trial as a witness for the prosecution. During the raid, one of the gang jumped on the counter and ran along until he came to Healey Harrison, the cashier. Pointing a gun at the man, he said: "Stand still, or you will get something through you." A second man then rifled the till. Harrison grabbed a £5 bag of silver and threw it at the robber. The cashier followed this with a cash shovel, which struck the man on the head. The raiders then attacked the bank officials, and a struggle ensued. Passers-by who heard the commotion called the fire brigade, and the men rushed into an adjourning room, demanding to be shown a safe way out.

"This was the worst bank which the accused could have chosen for the raid," said prosecuting counsel, "because it had no back exit, there being only a small heavily barred window, and they were caught like rats in a trap." Civilians came to the assistance of the bank clerks and guarded the door against the bandits. In the struggle, one escaped into the basement. He was pursued by a clerk, and locked in the strongroom until the arrival of the police. When the revolvers were examined later, two were found to be in perfect working order, and the third was loaded but would not fire. "It was only by the mercy of Providence that one of them did not go off," added counsel.

1934 – Public Enemy Era, Dillinger, Bonnie and Clyde

After temporarily blinding the clerk with pepper, a young man who raided the Great Moor (Stockport) branch of the District Bank on 14th February 1934 got away with about £50 in notes. While the clerk, Arthur Burgess, of Macclesfield, Cheshire, was having his lunch, he heard someone walk into the bank. On going to investigate, he was surprised to find a man behind the counter. He tried to grapple with him, but the intruder threw a packet of pepper in his face, jumped over the counter and ran away. No car was in sight at the time of the theft, and the only person, it seemed, who had seen anyone suspicious was a woman in a shop. The woman said that while she was having lunch she saw a man pass by her window. When he observed her, he pulled down the brim of his hat and ran away. The police took possession of a lead bludgeon which was found at the bank door, and they issued a description of the man, whom they said was about 28, dressed in a brown trilby hat and a light overcoat.

While bank raids were fairly uncommon in Britain at this time, they were a frequent nightmare for bank managers, clerks and law enforcement officials in the United States. Public enemy number one was a man named John Dillinger. On Sunday 4th March 1934, 50,000 militiamen together with policemen from Indiana, Ohio and Illinois formed an armed cordon with the object of trapping Dillinger. Known as "the Killer", Dillinger had escaped from jail on Saturday 3rd March after holding up 24 armed guards with a dummy pistol. He was last reported as being seen at Jacksonville, Illinois, apparently bound for Chicago.

The convicted criminal had locked the wardens in the prison, which had caused some amusement as well as exasperation and embarrassment in official circles. He seized the local female sheriff's car and then drove past 50 guards specially stationed around the prison to keep him safely inside. On hearing of his escape, Lillian Holley, the sheriff, became hysterical, and shrieked the news by telephone to police headquarters. "Send all the police guns you've got," she said. "Dillinger's loose."

It was reported that Holley was breathing vengeance against the dangerous fugitive. "If ever I see him again," she declared, "I will shoot him dead with my own pistol." The newspapers reported that she was a "crack shot". Reporting from Sioux Falls, Dakota, a day later, the question was: "Was John Dillinger, America's Public Enemy No. 1, who escaped from prison in dramatic circumstances last Saturday, the leader of an amazing bank raid here today?" Seven heavily armed bandits, one of whom was said to bear a close likeness to Dillinger, drove up to the Security National Bank, shot the policeman on guard and absconded with the contents of a safe. The actual robbery was accomplished by three of the bandits, who penetrated the president's office carrying machine guns, and commanded him to unlock the safe. Meanwhile, three other gang members – also armed with machine guns – stood guard at the door of the bank. Passers-by informed the police, and a police car dashed up to the bank. Machine guns were trained on the car, and the police were told to surrender or the bank raiders would fire. Caught in a trap, the police had little choice but to surrender as instructed. The crowd that had collected outside the bank quickly scattered when the gunmen fired their machine guns in the air. By this time, the other gang members had completed rifling the safe and joined the rest of the gang. They dragged two female bank clerks out with them and forced them to get inside a waiting car; they were then driven off as hostages. Police who chased the bank raiders were brought to a standstill with machine gun fire as the robbers used the hostages as shields. After a prolonged chase, the bank raiders escaped.

There was a new twist in the tale in mid-March 1934, following Dillinger's escape from the prison at Crown Point, Indiana. Herbert Youngblood, a companion of the fugitive, was seriously wounded at the time of the escape in a gunfight with the sheriff, as were three deputies. Although he was barely conscious, Youngblood gasped out some information about the gangster's whereabouts, which sent the authorities on an extensive manhunt through the suburbs of Port Huron. Youngblood later died. He had been arrested at a house in Southern Port Huron following a raid by police. Having opened the door to the police, he had immediately fired on them. Police returned the fire, causing fatal injuries. In hospital, the man's face was washed, and it was found that a scar on each cheek had been hidden by burnt cork. This led police officers to consider the possibility that Dillinger had been hiding out disguised as a black man. For some time, police, with the Assistant Prosecutor of the State and a shorthand writer, sat by the dying man's bedside. The night before he was shot, Youngblood said that he had spent the evening with Dillinger, who was driving a black coupé. They stayed at the injured man's bedside until he died, so that Dillinger couldn't get to him and stop him talking, and also to prevent a rescue attempt.

One month later, it was believed that "the Killer" was behind death threats received by George White, Governor of Ohio, if he did not reprieve two gangsters – friends of Dillinger's – who were awaiting death sentences. Both gangsters had been Dillinger's accomplices. The letter containing the threat was posted in Chicago and signed: "Friends of Harry Pierpont and Charles Makley." Pierpont and Makley, members of Dillinger's gang, were sentenced to death on 11th March 1934 for the murder of Sheriff Jesse Arber during Dillinger's escape from jail. Dillinger was also suspected to have masterminded a bank robbery which took place on 20th April 1934 at Pana, Illinois. Brandishing guns, four men had raided the Pana National Bank and decamped with more than $20,000.

Four days later, there were 20,000 men looking for Dillinger. All were heavily armed. Trapped in a roadhouse in Little Bohemia, Wisconsin, on 23rd April, Dillinger and his gang (including a woman) shot their way through 59 police, killing five and wounding 20 law officials. Dillinger and the woman raced away in a coupé, and the rest of the gang used another getaway vehicle. At St Paul, Minnesota, his car ran into an ambush laid by a sheriff and his men. Firing shots at the lawmen, Dillinger ran straight through the ambush. Hours later, said a telegram, the coupé was found abandoned 6 miles from the scene. The inside of the car was bloodstained, but there was no sign of the fugitive and his companion, who were believed to now be on foot. There was no sign of the other gang members either. The Wisconsin trap had been the most elaborate set for Dillinger, after someone had given his whereabouts to police. Police closed in on the roadhouse, while Federal agents dashed into the bar. However, watchdogs round the tavern betrayed their approach, and the gang were ready and waiting. The agents had barely crossed the threshold when the gang wheeled round as one, and opened fire.

By now, Dillinger's raids on banks had netted him thousands of dollars. He first struck the Security Bank in Sioux Falls, where he escaped with £5,000, before raiding the Manson City Bank on 13th March, getting away with thousands more. He then attacked a bank in St Louis, Florida, and took a further £2,000. He also raided a police station in Warsaw, Indiana, where he stole bulletproof waistcoats and guns.

On 5th May 1934, it was reported that Dillinger had fled to Britain, and was landing in Greenock on the CPR liner *Duchess of York*. The liner was due to visit Belfast before proceeding to Liverpool. An official of the shipping company in Liverpool stated that no news had been received at the offices of the company that Dillinger was on board. Inquiries at the ports also failed to obtain any confirmation. However, police in Britain were asked by Chicago police to watch for the fugitive among the passengers who disembarked. Dillinger was not spotted on the liner, and a couple of weeks later, Michigan police tried a new way of hunting America's most wanted man. He had already had native Americans with bows and arrows as well as cowboys using lassos on his trail, but now a plane was following his car. A bank in Flint, Michigan, was believed to have been raided by Dillinger and his gang on 18th May 1934, where they took £6,000. At this point, a police airplane was sent up to spot the bandits' car. A wireless message was sent to Central News informing them that the police believed they were trailing the car containing the gang. Things turned nasty again a week later, when Dillinger shot dead two policemen in East Chicago, Indiana, in an attempted bank robbery in a Chicago suburb. By this time, the governors of five states had posted rewards of £1,000 for his arrest.

On 26th May, it was reported that two policemen had been found in the front seat of their car with a dozen bullets in the neck of each man. All police posts were immediately put on watch, and suspicious cars were searched at various points along the main roads. Later that same day came the news that a gang member had been killed and another severely injured during an attempt to rob the bank in South Holland. Police connected the attempt with the murder of their colleagues.

Very little was heard of Dillinger until the following month, when it was reported that he was dead. Tommy Carroll, Dillinger's lieutenant, who was shot by police at Waterloo, Iowa, on 8th June 1934, declared from his hospital bed that his boss had died after escaping from police. When asked where Dillinger was buried, Carroll said: "I hid him." They were to be his last words. At this point, Federal agents were fairly convinced that the gangster had, indeed, died in an earlier shoot-out. But on 2nd July, it was revealed that just three days after Carroll's confirmation that Dillinger was dead, the man himself reappeared and carried out one of his most daring raids. The machine-gun-armed gang, robbed the Merchants National Bank at South Bend, Indiana, killing a policeman and wounding a bank customer and two bank officials before escaping with £5,000, after a running gun battle with the police in the streets. The gang sprayed the interior of the bank with machine gun fire when a clerk raised the alarm. They then used the vice-president of the bank and a clerk as shields to make their escape. Police barricaded all the roads in the area in an effort to capture the gang, and identified Dillinger as the leader of the raiders.

"The Killer" was back in the press two weeks later, when two policemen were wounded, one critically, in a shoot-out in Chicago. The two officers had tried to stop three cars for traffic violations, but were attacked by a volley of pistol shots. The wounded men were taken to hospital, and it was stated that at least one of the policemen would not survive. Unsurprisingly, the hunt for America's Public Enemy No. 1 was back on.

Two members of Dillinger's gang were being hunted by police in September 1934, after a daring plot was suspected in Denver,

Colorado. Denver police were warned that John Hamilton and Babyface George Nelson were plotting to intercept a gold shipment worth hundreds of thousands of dollars, which was being sent from San Francisco to the Denver Mint. Police were ordered to shoot to kill if any such attempt was made, and sharpshooters scoured the town seeking the pair, who were reputed to be equalled only by Dillinger, who by then had been gunned down. In October 1934, his successor, "Pretty Boy" Floyd, the "Phantom" bandit of Oklahoma, was mown down in a gun battle with police in Ohio. This just left Hamilton and Nelson as the most wanted gangsters in the United States. The year before, there had been 23 major gangsters; now there were just two.

"Ringed round with death and fighting like a tiger, Pretty Boy Floyd fell riddled with bullets ... at a farm near East Liverpool (Ohio) after exchanging shots with the police. He died shortly afterwards." Melvin Purvis, head of the Justice Department and the terror of criminals, who led the round-up that resulted in Dillinger's death, was cruising with 14 Federal agents through the woods when he spotted Floyd talking to two farmers near a farm, trying to induce them to take him to Youngstown, Ohio. The Federal agents leapt out of their cars and surrounded the gunman. Floyd started running across a bridge and Purvis shouted to him to halt, but as he ran on the agents fired 50 shots. On reaching Floyd, they found him holding a .45 calibre automatic in one hand, with another automatic in his holster. He was carried to the nearby farmhouse, where he died. Floyd had appeared there earlier in the day and asked for food.

After eating, he drew his automatic and ordered the farmer, Ellen Conckle's brother-in-law, to drive him to Youngstown. His death was the sequel to a number of dramatic events.

For the second time in a fortnight, he had escaped police custody in a shoot-out reminiscent of Dillinger. Like Dillinger, he was responsible for a number of murders, including those of six police officers, and more than 144 bank raids and kidnappings.

George Nelson – who following the deaths of Dillinger and Floyd became Public Enemy No. 1 – was believed to have been the leader of a gang which had shot its way out of a federal police trap near Barrington, Illinois, on 28th November 1934. A Federal agent was killed and another was seriously wounded in the gunfight. According to Reuter, Department of Justice officials were attempting to stop the car, which contained two men and a woman, when they were greeted by gunfire. They returned the fire, but the car sped on. Later, it crashed into another car, and three occupants were injured. The gang members drove on without stopping. It was known by this time that Nelson had sworn to avenge Dillinger's death, and Federal police were given orders to shoot him on sight, and shoot to kill.

The year 1934 was also when the notorious desperadoes Bonnie and Clyde were killed. On 23rd May, Clyde Barrow and Bonnie Parker, known as the "Cigar-smoking Girl Bandit", met sudden death in an 85mph gunfight with Texas Rangers. After a six-week search, a sheriff trapped the bandits in a house at Sailes, Louisiana, where he hid a squad of Texas Rangers in the bushes that lined the only road from the house. When Barrow passed in a car, travelling at around 85mph, "Like a bat out of hell", commented the sheriff, the official stepped into the middle of the road and ordered him to stop. Instead, Barrow "stepped on the gas", which was the signal for the rangers to open fire. Barrow was killed immediately, but Bonnie, who was smoking at the time, allegedly fired at the sheriff before she, too, was shot. The car careered out of control and crashed on an embankment. Both were found with machine guns on their laps, but they hadn't had a chance to get them into position. The back of the car was full of guns and ammunition. Barrow was, at this point, wanted for more than a dozen murders, kidnappings and bank hold-ups. He had been hunted by posses of police and sheriffs since 6th April 1934, when a constable was shot dead and a police chief kidnapped in Miami, Oklahoma. It was believed that the crime had been committed by Barrow and another gangster who had been liberated from jail by Bonnie and Clyde.

Interestingly, it seems that the story of these two gangsters, and the men who worked with them, would be forever immortalized when photos of the couple were found at an abandoned house. Barrow had certainly murdered police and civilians during his short stint as a gangster, but he mainly preferred to rob rural gas stations and the odd grocery store rather than banks. It seems that his connection to Bonnie Parker is what would make him one of those bandits hunted down during the United States' "Public Enemy" era. Bonnie was known to smoke Camel cigarettes, but it has been suggested that she never actually smoked cigars. Photos of her holding a cigar were found among the snapshots seized by police, and it is this, together with the fact that she was a young woman, which gave titillation to the story of Barrow. The public were presented with images of Bonnie and Clyde as lovers, fighting against all that was decent and right in society. Yet, although both had been to prison and Barrow was wanted for murder, there is no evidence to suggest that they slept together – Bonnie was actually married to someone else – or that she ever murdered anyone.

On 5th December, 1967, 12 white roses were laid on a lonely grave in Dallas, Texas. A middle-aged woman walked slowly away. Each and every month, for more than 32 years, the routine was repeated. The woman's name was Billie Jean Parker Moon. Buried in the grave was her sister, Bonnie Parker. On the grave, the epitaph read: "As the flowers are all made sweeter by the sunshine and the dew, so this old world is made brighter by the lives of folks like you." Clyde's gravestone, a few miles away, read: "Gone but not forgotten." Since her sister's death by machine gun fire, and the 26 bullets her body took, Billie Jean had remained tight-lipped about her sister. But, in 1967, at the age of 52, Billie Jean was ready to speak of the sister she had loved and gone to jail for.

"After Bonnie died," she said, "I was sentenced to 12 months for harbouring Bonnie and Clyde. But what would anyone have done? She was my elder sister and I loved her. You have no idea how I loved her. They let me out after nine months and I came home to Texas." As she spoke to a *Mirror* reporter, Billie Jean played constantly with a ring on the third finger of her left hand. "It belonged to Bonnie," she said. "Clyde bought it for her. It has 13 diamonds. Some folks were trying to cut her finger off to get at the ring as she lay dead in the car after the ambush. The coroner stopped them. He gave the ring to me. It hasn't been off my finger since.

"Bonnie was good and kind. She played the piano and wrote poetry and she took elocution lessons at school. She worshipped my mother. She was mother's pet. When Bonnie died, I believe a part of my mother died too. Some of the crimes she and Clyde were accused of were ridiculous. We used to read how they had robbed a bank and I knew it couldn't be true, because I had been with them at the time. They were always smart and well dressed. Bonnie used to buy her clothes in Kansas and Oklahoma. She had a wardrobe at home in Dallas and mother and I used to look after it for her. About once a month we would meet them somewhere in the country outside of town. The police watched the house and tapped our phone. But we worked out a secret system so that we could meet them.

"Clyde's father ran a filling station in Dallas. When they wanted to meet us, Bonnie and Clyde would drive slowly past the filling station and toss out a Coca-Cola bottle with a note inside saying where and when we were to meet. Mother and I would drive out and meet them in a field or on a country road. We used to take them fresh clothes and bring back Bonnie's dresses to be dry cleaned." Billie Jean then described how they took along baskets of food and had picnics. "They loved brown beans and chicken best," she said. Visits barely lasted more than half an hour – it was too risky.

"Sometimes we would take pictures of each other with Clyde's camera. There was one picture they had taken where Bonnie was pointing a shotgun at Clyde. But they were just joking," continued Billie Jean. "Bonnie got sick once, awful sick. She had been in a car crash and her leg was badly burned. I went to look after her in a motel in Arkansas and I stayed for three weeks. The burns were so severe that it took nine dollars worth of ointment a day to heal them."

Billie Jean smiled as she told of the night Bonnie and Clyde drove into Dallas. "She had a blonde wig and she put one of her dresses and the wig on Clyde. He had a fair complexion and with the wig was real feminine looking. Nobody ever guessed that he was really Clyde Barrow. We were always scared that one day they would be caught. Mama didn't live; she just existed while Bonnie was away. When we met she pleaded with her to come home. Bonnie told her: 'Mama, we've gone too far. They would put me in the electric chair.'" However, Billie Jean continues: "But I never heard Bonnie confess to anything. Sure, they were in gun battles, but I don't believe she ever killed anybody. When we met in motels, no one ever called anybody by their right name." Everyone was given a pet name.

It was the 1967 film *Bonnie and Clyde*, directed by Arthur Penn and starring Warren Beatty and Faye Dunaway, that brought about renewed interest in the couple, and led to Billie Jean's agreement to talk about her sister. "This film has brought the whole story back for me. It has made my life a hell. My husband's relatives didn't know who I was until this happened. Now some of them won't even speak to me." Billie Jean was suing Warner Brothers for more than $1m because she claimed the film was made "with utter disregard of her reputation, health and financial stability", and exposed her to "public hatred, contempt and ridicule". Billie Jean said: "Bonnie and Clyde were not thrill killers, you know. Why, once they took a policeman with them in Oklahoma. He stayed with them for four days and they didn't harm him. When they let him go, Clyde said: 'Bonnie, give him my best damn shirt.'" Whether Billie Jean's recollections, or the way in which her sister's story was portrayed to her, were deluded or false, and whether she really was the gun-toting moll that history has made her out to be, is not quite as clear cut as it could be. However, the fugitive herself said that the couple had gone too far, and whether or not she ever killed anyone, she certainly remained in the company of one of America's notorious killers, which ultimately led to death for them both.

Bonnie and Clyde, in reality, brought about the end of the Public Enemy era in the USA. Soon after the bank hold-ups and the killing spree in which 14 people died (most of them law enforcement officers), the United States brought in new laws that bank robbery and kidnapping were federal offences. By the summer of 1934, the growing coordination of the FBI, combined with the introduction of two-way radios in police cars began to make living as an outlaw or bandit incredibly difficult: certainly much more difficult than it had been for Clyde Barrow and Bonnie Parker. However, bank raids were still on the rise, and the UK was seeing its fair share.

On 27th November 1934, three armed men raided a branch

of Martins Bank in Cheetham, Manchester, after tying up the clerks. They escaped with £600. Just as the bank, on the junction of Elizabeth Street and Cheetham Hill Road, was about to close, the men entered the building and walked up to the counter. They threw pepper at the two clerks, then they drew their guns, and while one of them kept the clerks under surveillance the other two produced bandages and tied up their victims. After stuffing notes and coins into a black bag, they left the building, escaping in a saloon car with a Manchester registration number that was waiting in Elizabeth Street and sped off at high speed. The men did not tie the clerks up particularly securely, and even before the getaway car had started, one of them had freed himself and rushed out into the street. When the two clerks left the bank in the company of the branch manager, who wasn't present at the time of the raid, they stated that they had been advised by their head office not to divulge their names or any details of the raid. Neither of the men looked injured when they spoke to journalists shortly afterwards. The car used in the bank raid, which was hired, was found undamaged and abandoned in Stretford, on the western boundary of Manchester, on the Monday of the following week, and the steering wheel and other parts were taken by police to headquarters for examination by fingerprint experts. All roads around Stretford were under constant observation by patrols, and chief officers interviewed several people who it was stated, might be able to assist them. Two months later, and it was thought that the same gang were back at work.

1935 – Ruthless Gang Strikes Manchester Twice

On Friday 4th January 1935, a similar bank raid to the one carried out in November 1934 took place in Manchester. Three armed men escaped in a car with nearly £600 – after trussing up the bank manager and a clerk. The robbery was at a branch of the District Bank in Whittaker Lane, Heaton Park, and, again like the robbery in Cheetham Hill, it took place at around 3.00pm – the bank's closing time. So striking was the resemblance between the two raids that, although the hold-up occurred within the Lanes county police boundaries, Supts Valentine and Taylor of Manchester's CID were brought together to investigate. The three men who took part in the raid were believed to have spent a considerable time in the neighbourhood of the bank before they entered the building. Two of them went in as a woman was leaving. One produced a revolver and held up the manager, Mr Hammond, and his assistant, Mr Souter, while the other climbed over the counter, and, after binding the hands of both men with adhesive tape, gathered all the notes he could lay his hands on. A few minutes later, Mr Souter dashed into a shop next door but one to the bank, crying: "We have been raided." Lily Hilton, who was in the shop, cut him free, then ran into the bank and released Mr Hammond.

It was understood that the police believed the number plates on the car were false, and were the actual plates of a car that had been scrapped. Descriptions supplied by the two bank employees and by Mrs Hilton and the Revd Mr Hindley, the rector of St Hilda's Church, who noticed the men outside the bank before the raid took place, tallied with those that were issued by police following the Cheetham Hill raid. The police then tried to trace a maroon-coloured American saloon car, which was seen by at least a dozen people. The three raiders were all described as being in their mid-twenties, and of smart appearance.

It had "all the ingredients of an American gangster film", wrote a reporter in the *Mirror* just a fortnight later. "Bandits who jumped bank counters with guns in their hands ... Pepper thrown in the clerks' eyes ... Police who arrived just too late ... Raiders 'on a spree,' with girls ..." said the newspaper. They were referring to the court case in which three men were accused of two bank raids; this one in Cheetham Hill and another in Manchester. William Michael Kingham, 24, from Blackley, Manchester, Arthur Wood, 32, and Leo Kleva, 23, were accused of stealing £688 from a branch of Martins Bank at Cheetham Hill Road and using personal violence to two clerks, and robbing two clerks of £490 at the District Bank, Prestwich, in January when armed with an offensive weapon, and using violence on the clerks. In court, a young boy, William Hopkins, who had been standing in the doorway of a shop at the time of the first raid, said that three men got out of the car and two of them walked towards the bank. The third man was hailed by Hopkins, who mentioned that there was a cat on the axle of the car. Henry

Stansby, one of the bank clerks, told how at 2.58pm a man wearing a dark-coloured handkerchief over the lower part of his face entered the bank, with a gun in his hand, and jumped the counter. He stuck the gun into Stansby's chest and said: "Stick 'em up." The two other men then rushed into the bank. One covered the other clerk, Holmes, with a gun, and told him to put his hands up. The clerks then had pepper thrown in their faces, and as two of the perpetrators watched the clerks, the third man emptied the safe. Their hands and ankles were then bound with adhesive tape. Both Kleva and Wood were alleged to have met two girls later that night. They took them to a party, and told them they had robbed a bank that day.

The three accused, with handkerchiefs over their faces, then entered the District Bank on Whittaker Lane in Prestwich in January, shortly before 3.00pm. Each had a gun when they entered the premises, where they made a clerk hand over the keys to the safe. The two clerks were bound in exactly the same way as those in Cheetham Hill. In court, Winifred Turner and Margaret Holmes told how they had accompanied Kleva and Wood to Peover in Cheshire, where the men admitted to the robbery. The three men were remanded.

1937 - Temptation

"He says that he took a suitcase to the bank and filled it full of £1 and 10s notes, so far as he could judge to the extent of just over £10,000." These were the words of prosecuting counsel in the case of James Alfred Leslie Nicol, 38, from Hornchurch in Essex, who was committed for trial at the Old Bailey accused of theft. It was alleged that Nicol had stolen £10,071 from the Manor Park branch of Barclays Bank. At a previous hearing, Divisional DI John Harris stated that Nicol was taken into custody at Garstang in Lancashire.

Nicol had been a cashier at the Manor Park branch, and arrived unusually early on 27th March 1937. He left as usual at the end of the day, but did not report for work after the Easter holidays. Checks were made of his till, and the money was found to be missing. Nicol made a statement to the police in which he described that he was "suddenly tempted". He said: "I kept the case by my side until I left the bank, and I took it with me." The matter was reported in the newspapers when Nicol was committed for trial in July 1937, but a few days later, two men were arrested by Flying Squad officers late one night in connection with the stolen money. The men, the owner of a garage and a mechanic, were charged. Nicol was sentenced to two years after being found guilty of the crime. He was sentenced to hard labour at the Old Bailey. He had worked for Barclays for 17 years on a salary of £400 a year. On Easter Saturday 1937, he had arrived at work much earlier than usual. When Nicol was arrested, he only had £43 on his person. In his statement, the guilty man admitted that £5,700 was "in the hands of certain people". In court, it was stated that the married father of three was said to have developed a drinking problem. Meanwhile, the two other men were remanded in custody at East Ham. Walter Eberhard, 70, and Frederick Keiper, 43, were accused that "They did receive, comfort, harbour, assist and maintain" Nicol, knowing that he had stolen the money.

1947 – Heroics Beyond The Call of Duty

As the footsteps of six men sentenced to a total of 29 years in jail died away in Lord Chief Justice Goddard's court at the Old Bailey on 27th March 1947, there was an expectant hush. Then Lord Goddard said: "Stand up, Detective Sergeant Deans." William Deans, 37, stood up and faced the judge, with all eyes on him. Goddard continued: "The country, and London in particular, are most indebted to you for the extraordinary courage and devotion to duty you have shown in this case. You have added lustre to the already great record of the force to which you belong. I shall make it my duty to call the attention of the Secretary of State to your most commendable conduct." What had earned Deans this great tribute from the highest judge in the land was his heroism, a heroism that was beyond the line of duty. Three times, Dean had acted as a decoy for a gang of bank robbers. Each time, he knew he was likely to be kidnapped, maltreated, possibly even killed. On the third occasion, he was kidnapped, then sandbagged, flung into a lorry, and dumped to die, face down in the snow. To Deans it was "a bit of a job". But to his colleagues it was a task needing nerves of steel.

It was in February 1947 that Scotland Yard learned through the underworld of a plot to rob the Midland Bank, Kentish Town. Deans came forward as a volunteer, offering to impersonate the bank manager. So off came his police boots and on went the patent leather shoes. Some make-up and a pair of spectacles were applied, and he became the double of bank manager Mr Snell. On the night of 7th February, dressed as Snell, Deans locked the bank doors, took the tube to Woodside Park, Finchley (as the real Snell always did), and noted that he was followed by two men. They walked behind him to Holden Road, where a van drew up. In a house opposite, DI Crawford watched from a window through binoculars, while a female detective, Winifred Sherwin, hid against a fence. Deans steeled himself against the inevitable blow, but it never came: a policeman riding slowly by on his bicycle scared the bank raiders away. On the following Friday, the team went through the same performance. But, again, nothing happened.

On Friday 21st February, Deans was once again followed to Woodside Park, and this time was slugged with a sand-filled stocking, robbed of the bank's keys and flung, unconscious, into the waiting van. Unfortunately, the engine of the Flying Squad car which was in place to follow the van wouldn't start in the extreme cold weather, and the raiders were lost. Chief Inspector Lee, DI Crawford and Winifred Sherwin strolled up Kentish Town Road to the bank they knew was about to be robbed, walking arm in arm as if they were couples to avoid suspicion. The robbery was attempted, and the would-be bank raiders were arrested. William Deans was found later bound and gagged, face down in the snow at Barnet, Hertfordshire. Regaining consciousness, he crawled up to a house and told the stunned occupants: "Tell the Yard I've done it." Doris Deans said: "I am always telling my husband how brave he is ... but he doesn't like that sort of talk." However, it was reported that since the attempted robbery and his kidnap, Dean was having trouble sleeping, and suffered from raging headaches.

1950 – Robert Taylor and the George Cross

A young man was shot dead on 13th March 1950 when he grappled with a man who was being chased across Durdham Downs in Bristol. Richard "Bob" Taylor, 29, a single man from the Fishponds area of the city and a member of the advertising staff at the *Bristol Evening World*, was a keen athlete and an expert at judo. He joined a bus driver and conductor in the chase of two men who had earlier robbed a branch of Lloyds Bank and got away with £50. Taylor was seen to catch up with one of the men, whom he grappled with. Other pursuers, left behind by the pace of the chase, heard a gunshot and found Taylor dying: he had been shot through the head, and died later in hospital. A revolver was found nearby. Later, in a suburb, a squad car picked up two men, who were taken to Bristol police headquarters for questioning.

The following month, on 4th April, a Polish man, Roman Redel, was accused of murdering Taylor. "I don't believe it is true that I shot him. If I wanted to kill, I could have killed those two men in the bank, I had no wish to shoot anybody." Redel, 23, who was living in Bristol, was jointly accused alongside fellow countryman Zbigniew Gower, also 23, of murdering Bob Taylor. Prosecuting Counsel Mr Robey said that when Redel entered the bank – in North View – Mr Wall, the cashier, and Mr Bullock, the bank guard, were both on the premises. Redel, who was followed into the bank by Gower, pulled out a revolver and, pointing it at Bullock, said: "Stay where you are.

This is a hold-up." The bank raider then got Wall and Bullock into the manager's room, all the while pointing his gun at them. Gower climbed over the counter, rifled a drawer and stole £28 in notes, cheques and other documents. Both men then ran into the street. Mr Robey said that Bullock picked up a milk bottle and ran after the men. Redel again pointed the revolver at Bullock, telling him to stay where he was. Bullock threw his milk bottle, but missed. Several people had joined in the affray, among them Taylor, who outpaced all the others and nearly caught up with Redel. "But when Mr Taylor got within a few feet of him, Redel stopped, drew his revolver and fired a shot at point-blank range into Mr Taylor's face," said Robey. Redel's defence counsel, Hope Scott, applied that the case should not be tried in Bristol on the grounds that publicity was bound to have biased potential jurors. The magistrates agreed that the trial would be held in the Wiltshire Assizes, Salisbury, the following month.

On 25th May 1950, it was reported that Gower and Redel, both labourers, had been sentenced to death by the court for the murder of Bob Taylor. Counsel for Redel had tried to show the jury that the shooting was accidental, and that his client deserved a verdict of manslaughter. The jury recommended mercy for Gower, however. They were hanged at Winchester prison, four months later.

In August 1950, Bob Taylor was posthumously awarded the George Cross. Peter Scarman, the bus conductor, was awarded the George Medal, while Edward Cutler, the bus driver, was awarded the British Empire Medal (BEM). Fifty years after the fatal shooting of

Taylor, a blue plaque was placed on the family home where he had lived with his parents. Taylor, who had two older siblings, a brother and a sister, is the only Bristol resident who has ever received the George Cross. His death devastated his family.

1953 – Daring Raid on Canada House, London

After ringing the front door bell, six daring gangsters with a master plan broke into the "burglar proof" Canada House in London's West End on 8th February 1953. It was one of the most cool-headed raids ever committed. The gangsters chose a five-storey, fortress-like building, heavily guarded by burglar alarms and steel doors. Canada House – an office block including the headquarters of the Canadian Government – was conspicuously placed on an island site, close to Scotland Yard.

Throughout the night, the gang calmly set about trying to blast open vault doors with explosives. The gang, carrying explosives in a suitcase, walked up to the main door and rang the bell late on a Saturday night. A night watchman who answered was overpowered and tied up, and his keys were taken from him. The gang had made a careful study of the layout of the building, and the first thing they did was to lock the watchman in a room without a telephone. Then they went into the offices of the Royal Bank of Canada, where many thousands of pounds were held secure in the basement vaults. This was their target. All night they blasted the double-grilled doors with gelignite charges, but the doors stood firm. The men then turned their attention to two safes, blowing them open by putting explosives in the keyholes and then covering them, before lighting a flex attached to a reading lamp. However, at that point the plan went wrong. There was very little money in the safes. In the adjoining offices of the Sun Life Assurance of Canada, they also found little money: altogether, they had less than £1,000. While the gang were still at work, the main doorbell rang. It was the relief watchmen. The gang released the first watchman and forced him to open the door. As he did so, they pulled in the second watchman, took them both inside and locked them in a room. At around 11.00am, hours after the gang had left, one of the watchmen struggled free from the ropes that he had been tied with. He pushed himself up to a window on the second floor, overlooking Cockspur Street, and bellowed for help.

Dennis Champion, 23, selling Sunday newspapers opposite the bank, heard the cries. He ran about 30yds to Trafalgar Square, where there were two policemen on the beat. One returned to the bank while the other phoned Scotland Yard. Five minutes after the alarm, when squad cars arrived, police didn't know how to get through the bank's thick 14ft 3in high bronze and brass double doors, secured by four locks and chains. The police finally entered after Canadian officials in cars arrived with keys. At 9.00pm, DS Tom Barratt, one of the "Big Five", left the bank with a squad of officers, having been there all day. Detectives found a fingerprint on the inside of one of the blown safes, and the two night watchmen were taken to Cannon Row police station, where they were shown photographs from the Yard's Rogues Gallery.

1955 – A Trusted Customer and the Bank He Raided

Leonard Warren told police that he robbed a bank of £23,800 and gave the money to two men. However, the court was told, on 11th August 1955, that he might not have been speaking the truth. DS Orange was opposing bail for Warren, 38, from Coventry. Warren had claimed that he drove off from the Cosford Green branch of Lloyds Bank after stealing the money from a car and handing it to two men. The money was still missing at this point, and Orange felt that, should Warren be allowed bail, police inquiries might be hindered. Bail was refused.

Warren had been a trusted customer at the bank. In fact, he had been so trusted at the branch that one day the manager asked him to take £23,800 in his car to the bank's head office: the regular messengers were on holiday. The money, said Mr Kenderline, prosecuting, was carefully placed in the boot of Warren's car. Suddenly, he drove off, leaving some very surprised bank clerks behind. Warren, a motor engineer, appeared in court accused of stealing the money. Kenderline said that soon after the money was stolen, Warren walked weeping into a police station. He said that he drove off with the cash because he was being blackmailed over his friendship with a "high society" woman. In his statement, the accused said: "I set off to go to the bank. A bloke I had seen once or twice before flagged me down. He asked if I knew a particular woman. He told me the full history of my association with her. I had packed her up and forgotten about her. He said he wanted the money and if I didn't deliver it, he would spill the beans."

In the alleged statement, Warren added that he later drove to meet the man. "This man and another put the money in a car and drove off." DS Robert Orange told the court that Warren, a married man, would say no more about the woman. He said: "It is too big. She is too high in society. If I tell you, the London boys will get at the wife and kids." He also faced other charges of either stealing or receiving, and was sent for trial. He pleaded not guilty on all counts.

Described as "poker-faced", Leonard Warren was back in the news in November 1955, when it was reported that he had been sent to jail for five years. Known to police as the Human Oyster, because of his 11-minute secret, it was revealed that during the short time he had the money it vanished in broad daylight close to Coventry's city centre. No trace of the banknotes had been found. Only one man knew the answer to the riddle – and Warren refused to talk to anyone about it, even his wife. In the lounge of the couple's bungalow at Princethorpe in Warwickshire, Sally Warren, 32, told the *Mirror*: "I am as puzzled as you. I know some people are whispering that I must know more about it, but in all the times I visited my husband in prison, he never allowed me to mention the subject."

Warren had stood calm and erect in the dock at Coventry Quarter Sessions as he was sentenced for the theft of the money.

He pleaded guilty in the end. He stole the money when he'd agreed to take it for the bank manager, by driving off with a suitcase containing the notes, while leaving the bank clerk – who was to have accompanied him – behind on the street. Just a few minutes later, he stopped a motorist and asked to be taken to a police station. Since then, squads of detectives had searched the area without success. His story of blackmail by two men was rejected by the court recorder.

In March 1959, bank robber Len Warren walked briskly from a railway station and joined his wife Sally in the couple's family car. The last time he had been in the mud-spattered vehicle was when he had driven off with the money. His five-year sentence had been reduced for "good conduct remission". He had been in prison in Leyhill, Gloucestershire, and travelled from there by train to Coventry. He was then driven to the family home, where he still refused to talk about what had happened to the money. With a solicitor at his side, he quietly insisted: "What is in the past is in the past. I made a statement to police at the time." In his absence, the couple's bungalow had been surrounded by a 22-acre smallholding, including costly stables and poultry pens. They certainly weren't there before he went to jail.

However, the dream life wasn't to last. On 27th March 1961, Warren was jailed for a further 12 years after being dubbed "The Brains" of a six-man gang known as "The Ringers", who had stolen £16,000-worth of cars in nine months, which he "disguised" before selling them. His 12-year sentence was imposed at Birmingham

Assizes. For a week, the jury had heard a story that was just like a programme on television at the time. Warren had arranged for wrecked cars to be bought, and their number plates and logbooks transferred to stolen cars which matched them. Warren was arrested in Ireland after skipping bail. Mr Justice Stevenson told him: "You were unwise enough to recruit some very clumsy lieutenants." After sentencing him for conspiring to steal cars, the judge jailed the five other men for car theft and conspiracy. They were Derek Cockayne, 23, John Stanford, 21, Derek Henley, 26, Thomas Denne, 22, all of whom received three years in jail, and William Bridgeman, who received two years.

Back in 1955, a man with his face covered in a raincoat was escorted from a train by detectives at King's Cross station. He was taken by car to Scotland Yard. The man, George Grey, 56, had been detained by police at Middlesbrough in Yorkshire, where it was considered that he answered the description of a monocled major wanted for questioning in connection with a safe-blowing robbery in London. The same man was wanted for a £44,000 bank robbery in Glasgow. At Middlesbrough, a few minutes after the train left, a woman rushed to the platform by taxi. Grey meant a great deal to 35-year-old recently widowed Gladys Fairweather.

George Grey was soon tucked safely away in jail, serving 13 years for bank robbery and safe cracking, and thinking that all his possessions were as safe as he was. When he was released from Edinburgh jail in 1964, after serving nine years of his sentence, he immediately launched a £750 claim against Glasgow police.

"According to Grey," said his solicitor, Colin MacRae, "the police have said that the clothing [they had in suitcases at Glasgow police station] was destroyed by a plague of moths. Several suitcases of clothing and personal effects had been held by the police after his arrest." It transpired that for some months before his release, Grey had been negotiating with police for their return. The chief constable neither admitted or denied the point about the moths in the letter in which he replied to Grey's request for compensation. Australian George Grey married widow Gladys Fairweather in November 1964.

Just one month before that wedding, two young bank officials, an accountant and a clerk with a degree in sciences, decided that there was more money in robbing a bank than working for one. They planned what a judge hailed as: "An ambitious scheme which, if successful, might have made them rich for life." The clerk, Ronald Littlewood, 31, a native of Leeds living in London, and Gillies Lister, 22, originally from Scotland but living in Kensington, worked in the same London bank. An expert crook told them that on Monday nights there was always £40,000 in the strongroom of a Dublin bank. Littlewood went on holiday to Dublin, and during banking hours took a look at the strongroom. He then returned to London. Later, both men sailed for Dublin, hired a car, rented a cottage by the sea and bought tools for the bank raid. They also acquired watertight containers in which to bury the stolen money under a rock on the coast near Howth.

The two bank officials turned bank robbers forced a window at the bank, bored a hole in the door of the strongroom and packed it with gelignite. They lit a fuse – then drove round the block, timing their drive so that they returned immediately after the explosion. But they found it had only made a small hole, so they set another charge and went out for another drive. This time, a policeman was waiting outside. While he was talking to the two men, the second charge went off, so he arrested them. DS Edmund Garvey told the Dublin Circuit Criminal Court the story when Littlewood was sentenced to three years in prison and Lister to 18 months.

What the policeman did not say in court was that on the night that they carried out their carefully planned raid, every bank in Dublin was being watched. Police had been tipped off that a known bank robber was likely to make an attempt on some bank in the city.

1956 – Two Britons Held in France, While Germany Witnesses Shooting

French police arrested two Britons who, it was alleged, held up a female bank cashier at the then fashionable Juan-les-Pins, on the French Riviera. They managed to grab £350 in franc notes. The Britons, brothers Jack, 31, and Francis Hobbs, 29, came from Luton. Josette Ramaioht said: "I was serving alone in the bank. Two Englishmen were last in a queue of tourists changing money. When the other tourists had gone, one Englishman said: 'Hand over your cash,' and grabbed me by the throat through the open cash window. The other seized the money on my counter. They ran out, I followed, screaming." The Hobbs brothers were charged with robbery and assault. Police said that the brothers told them that they had spent their money but wanted a longer holiday.

However, in Germany things were less straightforward. A 14-year-old American boy found himself in the middle of a real-life drama on 19th September 1956. Robert Kuhel was captured by an armed bandit, but turned the tables when he shot the man dead. The story began when Hugo Waigenbach called at the Kuhels' home in Heidelberg at 9.30am. He pulled out a pistol and demanded that Robert's father, John Kuhel, who was the manager of the Heidelberg branch of an American bank, should go to his office and hand over

£25,000. Robert asked to be excused, went into the bathroom and slipped his father's 0.22 automatic into his pocket. Then, with his father driving, he, his mother and the bank raider set off in the family car for the bank.

Waigenbach's plan was to hold Robert and his mother in the car outside the bank while John Kuhel went in for the money. Robert waited for his chance, and when his father swerved the car he pulled out the automatic weapon and shot the robber in the head. The man died instantly.

1957 – Drama, Death and Mental Illness in West Germany

A verdict was expected in the German murder trial of British man, Brian Cowell, 31, on 11th November 1957; he was accused of shooting a policeman. Cowell, from Orpington, Kent, if found guilty, would only face a life of imprisonment, as West Germany had no death penalty. He admitted during the trial at Mannheim that he shot at the policeman while carrying out a bank robbery during the summer. Alongside Cowell was another accused man, Kurt Schuler, 27, from Germany.

Experts said in evidence that the bullet that killed the policeman – Constable Ruecher – came from Cowell's gun. Three other bullets which had come from Schuler's gun were relatively harmless, they said. The seven jurors, including one woman schoolteacher, retired to consider their verdict.

A murdered call girl, known as "Blonde Rosemarie", was mentioned in court during the trial, which caused a moment of surprise. Public Prosecutor Dr Hans Zwicker asked Schuler: "Did you ever associate with Rosemarie Nitribitl – better known as 'Blonde Rosemarie' of Frankfurt?" The call girl, who was the associate of wealthy businessmen, had been found strangled a fortnight earlier in her luxury apartment in Frankfurt. At the time of her death, Schuler, who said he did know her, was in jail on remand. Dr Zwicker asked: "Did you ever give her money?" Schuler replied: "No. I only knew her slightly because she stopped her car as she passed me in the street and spoke to me." Later, in his final speech, Dr Zwicker demanded sentences of life imprisonment for both Schuler and Cowell. He said the two men were "ice-cold criminals". Apart from the main murder charge, Cowell and Schuler were also accused of attempting to murder another policeman, and of bank robbery. During the trial, the two men had admitted robbing a Mannheim bank of around £4,000. Dr Hans Hoffman, the Mannheim prison doctor, told the court that Cowell came from a middle-class family, but there was a history of suicide on his mother's side. Schuler appeared to have a stronger personality then Cowell, the doctor said. He added: "Cowell told me he could not bear to have his mother present." His father, a retired civil servant, and his mother who lived in Bognor, Sussex, had, however, visited their son in prison in Germany.

Cowell's dreams were shattered on 12th November 1957 when he was given a sentence of life imprisonment with hard labour. He was found guilty of murder. Both Cowell and his German accomplice, Schuler, who was also sentenced to life imprisonment, pleaded that they did not shoot to kill. They were told that they had a right to appeal on legal grounds. Behind his glasses, Cowell's red-rimmed eyes blinked a few times as the black-robed judge read the court's verdict. It was his bad eyesight and his spotty complexion that had given the 31-year-old the inferiority complex that turned him into a criminal, the court was told.

Cowell had wanted to be a big shot, but no one had taken him seriously. So he gave himself a big build up. To his friends, he posed as an ex-public schoolboy, whereas in actual fact he went to a high school in Westcliff-on-Sea, Essex. He said he had been a restaurant owner in Canada, but had only ever worked as a waiter in a restaurant in Montreal. He said he was a well-travelled Romeo, yet the only girls who ever associated with him where those he had picked-up at nightclubs, and call girls. After emigrating to Canada in 1952, he wrote to his parents telling them what a success he had become. In fact, he and his friend Schuler were walking the streets penniless. They moved on to the USA, where they took odd jobs, then earlier in 1957, they had travelled to Germany, where they soon became penniless again. The duo turned their attentions to bank robberies. From one raid they escaped with £750. Then came the fatal raid at the Mannheim bank, in which Cowell shot a policeman as they tried to make their getaway. The judge, Dr Hermann Huber, summed up the two guilty men when he said: "Two men who did not want to be Mr Nobody – but wanted to reap what they had not sown."

The following year, in April, the West German Supreme Court ordered a retrial for both men on the murder and armed robbery charges. The court ruled that legal mistakes had been made in the trial in November 1957. But the verdict returned was the same for Cowell – life imprisonment with hard labour. The appeal had failed, but Cowell vowed to fight on.

In August 1964, Cowell's parents made a dramatic appeal on

CASSIDY AND CO.: The gang in formal mood (left to right) The Kid, Bill Carver, Ben Kilpatrick, Harvey Logan, Cassidy.

1908 – Butch Cassidy The infamous Butch Cassidy (front right) with fellow gang members the Sundance Kid, Bill Carver, Ben Kilpatrick and Harvey Logan. Following a series of bank robberies – including a $32,000 haul from Nevada – it was alleged that they were shot and killed by Bolivian soldiers in 1908.

SCOTTISH BANK CASE

1922 – Granton Bank William Stewart (centre) was sentenced to eight years imprisonment for his involvement in the theft of £20,000 of Canadian Grand Trunk Pacific bonds from Granton Bank in 1922.

SUSPECTED BANK RAIDERS' ARREST

1925 – Swindon The getaway car stolen from Harley Street and believed to have been used in a bank raid in Swindon. Divisional Inspector Ward found himself in the firing line when attempting to arrest the two suspects – James Walsh and John O'Sullivan.

1926 – Portsmouth The scene of an early 20th-century bank raid, Lloyds Bank in Portsmouth, where John Thurston was accused of robbing William Mountford (right) before Sergeant Hopkinson (left) intervened.

Police Constable Harold Clark, who was shot

Mr. John Stevenson, a labourer, severely injured in the head.

Mr. R. H. Vipond, aged 67, gardener, shot in the chest.

Mr. Thomas Drew, who seized McAllister and with the help of others got him to the ground.

Following the raid by an armed man at the District Bank, Great Homer-street, Liverpool, and the shooting of a policeman and three civilians, William McAllister, an Irish Free State ex-soldier, aged twenty, was remanded yesterday on charges of shooting and robbery. When charged he said: "I did not take aim at them."

1934 – John Dillinger Serial bank robber John Dillinger was America's public enemy number one in the mid-1930s.

An upper window from which John Dillinger — America's public enemy No. 1 — jumped to escape police near Mercer, Wisconsin.

Window panes shattered by bullets at Little Bohemia roadhouse, where Dillinger fought the police.

This series of photographs shows how Dillinger evaded police in Wisconsin. He finally met his match during a shoot-out in Chicago on 22nd July 1934, succumbing to gunshot wounds inflicted by FBI agents.

1934 – Bonnie and Clyde Two more of America's most notorious bank robbers met their death in 1934, when Bonnie Parker and Clyde Barrow (pictured) were finally tracked down by a group of Texas Rangers in Louisiana.

Clyde Barrow armed with two shot-guns.

1935 – Manchester Mr Hammond, manager of the Heaton Park branch of the District Bank in Manchester, leaves the scene of the crime in a police car. He and assistant Mr Souter were bound with tape during the robbery.

Mr. H. H. Hammond, manager of the bank, leaving in a police car after the raid.

Before the introduction of computers, locating the relevant information could be a long, laborious job, as this 1947 shot of Scotland Yard's central records office clearly demonstrates.

The 1950s saw more than its fair share of bank raids. Here's a snatched shot of a crime scene, with detectives from Scotland Yard at St Martin's Bank, Piccadilly Circus. Bank clerks arrived at the bank in February 1955 to find the safe had been blown open and its contents missing.

LEN WARREN

1955 – Coventry Len Warren was a trusted customer of Lloyds Bank in Cosford Green, Coventry until August 1955. The bank's regular messengers were on holiday, so the manager asked him to drive £23,800 in bank notes to the city's main branch in his car. The money disappeared, and Warren – later nicknamed "the human oyster" and "the brains" – served five years in prison.

1955 – Glasgow George Grey was jailed in 1955 for his part in a £44,000 bank robbery in Glasgow, but the "monocled major" had the cheek to sue the Glasgow police for £750 on his release nine years later, because, he claimed, his clothes had been destroyed by moths while in storage.

1957 – Kingston Despite the best efforts of safe manufacturers, criminals always seemed to find a way to get inside. This safe in Kingston's Lloyds Bank had been covered in egg boxes and sacking to deaden the sound of the explosives used, and the raiders got away with an estimated haul of £46,000 in cash and jewels in December 1957.

1958 – Donald Hume Donald Hume, pictured in January 1958, served eight years in prison for being an accessory to murder. Knowing that he could not be tried for the same crime twice, he confessed upon his release that he was the actual murderer, and re-enacted the crime for the press and monetary gain. Hume went on to rob the Midland Bank in London in August 1958, among others, and was eventually sentenced to life imprisonment.

1958 – Cranbrook Martin Searby – allegedly desperate for notoriety – was jailed for five years after holding up Lloyds Bank in Cranbrook at gunpoint and stealing £2,274, in March 1958.

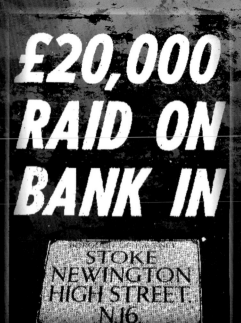

£20,000 RAID ON BANK IN

STOKE NEWINGTON HIGH STREET. N.16.

1958 – Stoke Newington Robbers gained entry to the Stoke Newington High Street branch of Midland Bank by cutting the bars on a basement window. The raid in London saw the gang use specialist equipment to cut through the 9in thick "burglar-proof" steel door of the strongroom to escape with £20,000 in October 1958.

Ada Shakeshaft (left) was one of those accused of taking part in the Stoke Newington robbery, but it was decided that there was not enough evidence to send her to trial. She was, however, charged with receiving some of the stolen money.

Daily Mirror
FORWARD WITH THE PEOPLE
No. 17,090

MANHUNT

50,000 POLICE SEEK MR. BROWN

—He may hold clue to bank shooting

By TOM TULLETT, Chief of the Mirror Crime Bureau

THE giant police hunt for Donald Brown, 39, became world-wide yesterday when Scotland Yard called in Interpol, the international police organisation.

This was done because Brown, the man Scotland Yard wish to interview in connection with the Midland Bank shooting at Brentford, Middlesex, once spent some time in Paris, and is known to have friends abroad.

By last night every one of the 50,000 police in Britain had been issued with descriptions and pictures of Brown.

CID Men Swoop on Clubs

In London, detectives swooped on West End clubs and restaurants. Brown is known to be fond of visiting night clubs.

They also visited a number of houses in the Chelsea, Kensington and Shepherds Bush districts of London.

These moves followed a flood of telephone calls to the Yard during the week-end, from people who said they knew Brown.

The Yard based his description on features because they believe he may be able to help their inquiries into the bank hold-up, twelve days ago, in which a man was shot and wounded the manager, Mr. Eric Alves.

It was the second time in three

THE MEN WHO WERE SHOT
Bank manager Eric Alves, who was wounded by a two-gun bandit in this month's bank raid.
Cashier Frank Lewis. He was wounded in a raid which took place at the same bank last August.

months that the Brentford branch of the bank had been raided.

Last August a gunman held up the staff and wounded a cashier, Mr. Frank Lewis.

The loot from that raid was £2,300 and in the second robbery only £200 was taken.

Brentford Vital believe that the same man was responsible for both hold-ups.

A bank assistant, Miss Margaret Kirby, got a close look at the gunman on each occasion.

Her Address Is Secret

She has told police that she will be able to recognise him again.

A police guard on Miss Kirby has been strengthened. She has been transferred to another branch of the bank and police have asked for her address to be kept secret.

The reason for Brown is one of the biggest carrying out in Britain for years.

Last night police were making and checks at various and his address and anti-climactic very strong all over Britain.

All police reports have been warned to watch for Brown so he is able to fly away places.

The Yard description says he is believed to be in possession of two firearms.

This is how they describe Brown:—

> 5ft. 7in. tall, stoutly built, with dark brown hair. Has a round face, ruddy complexion, fat lips and grey eyes, frequently smiling. Usually smartly dressed and sometimes uses an American accent.

Although Scotland Yard do not care their statement he changed his name to Donald Brown some months ago by deed poll. He also does an alias—John van der...

Brown is an electrician by trade and nine works may be run verified on a lot at Welwyn Garden City, Herts.

POLICE GUARD HER
Police watch on Miss Margaret Kirby (above) has been strengthened. She is the bank girl who can identify the Brentford bank gunman.

WHO IS YOUR CHOICE?
For the Mirror's New Year Honours List—See Page 6

1958 – Brentford The *Daily Mirror* breaks the news that in November 1958 50,000 police were searching for the gunman who carried out an armed robbery at Brentford's Midland Bank.

By the end of the 1950s, banks were striving to make it harder for thieves to target them and their money. In November 1958 this bank official demonstrates a new type of bank bag that if stolen will detonate a smoke and dye bomb, thereby destroying the bank notes within.

1959 – London A detective clears out equipment left by bank raiders during an attempted robbery at the Commercial Street, Stepney, branch of Midland Bank.

Dennis Cashman, on his first day in his new job as a special weekend security patroller, foiled the gang's plans to snatch an estimated £30,000.

1960 – Birmingham Nicknamed "Prince of the Peter Boys" by detectives, the debonair James Hulme Milne was sentenced to 10 years in jail for his part in stealing more than £27,000 from Barclays Bank, Bordesley, Birmingham, in September 1960.

1960 – Bayswater, London
An artist's diagram of Barclays Bank at Queensway, Bayswater, with part of the wall cut away to show how the bandits made a hole in the ceiling to gain entry to the bank in November 1960.

1960 – Durrington
Victor Terry and Valerie Salter arrived in London having been arrested in Glasgow in November 1960. Terry was sentenced to death for the murder of a caretaker-guard during a bank raid at the Durrington, Sussex branch of Lloyds, while Salter received probation despite being found guilty of being an accessory after the fact.

Along with Terry and Salter, the other two involved in the crime were Alan Hosier (who was found guilty of non-capital murder and sentenced to life imprisonment) and Philip Tucker (who was only 16 at the time of the incident, and so was ordered to be detained at Her Majesty's pleasure).

I CONFESS !

AFE - BREAKER Donald
Mather couldn't forget his
part in a bank robbery.
The guilty secret preyed on his
mind more and more as time went

Finally he walked into a police
station and confessed — FOURTEEN
YEARS after the raid.

For that time, Worcester Crown
Court heard yesterday...

Robber owns up after 14 years

By MIRROR REPORTER

MATHER: Bank raid in 1964

1964 – Kidderminster Donald
Mather was a rarity in terms of bank
robbers. Having succeeded in snatching
£24,000 from the strongroom of
Kidderminster's National Provincial
Bank in June 1964, his conscience got
the better of him, and he confessed to
the crime in August 1978.

The introduction
of closed-circuit
television
(CCTV) in
London in
January 1968
proved a vital
tool in tracking
criminals'
getaway
vehicles
following
bank raids.

Yard name the
three men on
the run with
mystery girl

Roger Louis Dewhurst   Terence John Thorne   Christopher Hogan

ARMED CID TIGHTEN NET ON CAR GANG

By TOM TULLETT and SID GRANT

Farmer's
jailed
killers
'want to
marry'

1968 – Birmingham Three
fugitives wanted for armed
robbery were named by
Scotland Yard detectives in
December 1968.

MIRROR CRIME BUREAU

BRITAIN'S FIVE MOST WANTED MEN

1970 – Cornhill, London Following an armed raid on the Cornhill branch of the National Westminster Bank in the heart of the City of London in November 1970, in which Securicor guard Raymond Harden was murdered, the police issued photofit images of the five most wanted men in Britain.

Mirror

GUN GANG FLEE IN HIJACK CARS

Night chase after bandits shoot PC

1971 – Gravesend Police Constable Peter Dinsdale in hospital in Maidstone in March 1971. He attempted to apprehend a gang who had raided the National Westminster Bank in Gravesend, but had ammonia squirted in his face before being shot in the leg.

1971 – Baker Street Police inspect the burglar alarm at Lloyds Bank, Baker Street, in September 1971. Because the robbery was overheard by a radio ham operator, the episode became known as the Walkie-Talkie Bank Raid.

Police officers stand guard at the crime scene. The robbers rented a leather goods shop named Le Sac, two doors down from the bank, and tunnelled a distance of approximately 50ft (15m), passing under the intervening Chicken Inn restaurant. To avoid being overheard, they only dug during weekends.

The inquisition continued to rumble on for months, with the police having to defend their actions and their failure to prevent the robbery.

1975 – Bank of America This artist's reconstruction clearly shows how the raiders gained entry to the Bank of America's vault in April 1975, to escape with a staggering £2m haul.

ON INNOCENT SOULS

HE WAS SO COOL SAYS THE CABBIE

TAXI-DRIVER Lawrie Henriques was an unsuspecting accomplice on one of the crooked parson's most daring raids.

Without knowing it, Lawrie was the getaway driver when Stephen Care grabbed priceless vestments from the Roman Catholic Buckfast Abbey, on the edge of Dartmoor.

The 51-year-old cabbie, who lives in Torquay, said:

Sorry

Just as a joke I asked him if he'd done a job. He told me he was just borrowing some stuff. He showed me round the abbey grounds.

Lawrie said he always drove the parson at cut-price fares because he felt sorry for him.

The taxi man added: "Once when we were travelling ...

THE V I P: Stephen Care presenting prizes at Greylands School in Paignton. He later called back . . . to steal antiques. On the left is Mrs. Dorothy O'Brien, who brought about the clergyman's downfall when she spotted some of the haul in a shop.

1976 – Biddy and Clyde The Revd Stephen Care presents prizes to pupils at Paignton's Greylands School. He returned to steal antiques, which he then sold, but his most audacious crime was a raid on the Southway branch of Lloyds Bank in Plymouth.

Care's accomplice in crime was his frail 58-year-old housekeeper Stella Bunting. The press dubbed them Biddy and Clyde.

His crimes .. and the spoils

BIDDY AND CLYDE —BANK RAIDERS EXTRAORDINARY

HARDENED detectives were stunned by the "Biddy and Clyde" bank robbery.

Two unlikely raiders broke just about every rule in the criminal book. Yet they made a clean get-away with £1,775 in cash.

CLYDE was crooked curate Stephen Care. He masterminded the audacious raid on Lloyds Bank in Southway, Plymouth.

BIDDY was his frail and deaf housekeeper, 58-year-old Stella Bunting.

When the clergyman outlined his plan to Mrs. Bunting at the vicarage in Paignton, he told her: "Come on, we're going to rob a bank." The simple-minded housekeeper was far from keen.

"That wouldn't be right for a clergyman," she protested.

But the persuasive curate replied: "Non-sense. We shall be like Robin Hood, robbing the rich to feed the poor."

The housekeeper was convinced. And off they went to the bank by taxi.

Care wore the most ridiculous of disguises—an Andy Capp flat hat, a false moustache, and a piece of sticking plaster over his nose.

But he got into the bank manager's office before he announced...

BIDDY: Housekeeper Stella Bunting

...bomb in the building and could trigger it by a transmitter in his pocket.

Care was handing over. And the quaint couple retreating to their waiting taxi.

The bank raid last summer was Stephen Care's most spectacular escapade in a two-year crime spree.

It all began in December, 1973, when he got an easy £700 insurance payout by claiming that his vicarage had been robbed. Then he raided five homes and picked up antiques and other items worth £1,500.

...came next, when he snatched £12,000-worth of gem-studded vestments from Buckfast Abbey.

This was followed up by the bank raid in Plymouth.

Then the light-fingered clergyman cleaned out £1,500-worth of antiques from Greylands School in Paignton.

That was when detectives began closing in. But the curate stole on, filling his pockets.

Just before he was arrested he snaffled £55 from the funds of a new church—St. Chad's in Plymouth...

The latter decades of the 20th century saw the police using the latest technology in their attempt to crack down on bank raids and other crimes. Chief Inspector Jack Ashman, Superintendent Castree, Chief Superintendent John Lawton, Superintendent Jim Heywood and Assistant Chief Constable Ron Thompson show off their latest £5m centralized control room system in January 1980.

behalf of their son, asking the West German government to send their son back to Britain. Cowell had been kept in prison until April 1963, but by the time of his parents' appeal he was under psychiatric care in a civilian hospital near Heidelberg. The couple wanted Cowell to be allowed to move to a British hospital. A British Rhine Army psychiatrist, who saw Cowell earlier in 1964, reported that he was suffering from a serious mental illness. In Bonn on 29th August, a government spokesman said that the appeal by Edward and Clara Cowell was being studied. Cowell's mother, who had last seen her son at Christmas 1963 said: "I believe that once back in Britain ... he could be cured. It would be wrong for the Home Office to send him to Broadmoor. I don't feel he would get the right treatment there. But if the German authorities make it a condition of our son's release that he should be sent to Broadmoor, then we must accept." On 14th December 1964, it was announced in the Commons that Cowell would be released from jail and deported. "Because of his mental condition, the government is ready to make the appropriate arrangements," said Walter Padley, Minister of State for Foreign Affairs.

Just three days after Cowell was found guilty of armed robbery and murder in West Germany, things were rather different in Hounslow. Unlike Cowell, who was still using a "smash and grab" method – reminiscent of the first half of the century's hold-ups both in the United States and Britain – a new kind of bank raider was coming to the fore. The new gangs were organized, well-informed and vigilant. A well-planned operation under the cover of darkness brought much greater riches than a few notes grabbed from the cashier's counter. As an example, a silent gang took six hours to blast their way into a bank's strongroom and safe on 15th November 1957. The reason they took so long was because they spent so much time muffling the gelignite explosions. Their haul was £40,000 in cash and jewellery. It was a "brilliant" raid, said a police officer. The gang arrived between 9.00 and 10.00pm to begin their invasion of the National Provincial Bank in Hounslow's High Street. Police also arrived at the time, with the aid of a barking dog. The silent thieves must have made some noise as they climbed over walls to get to a rear window of the bank. Dorothy Vanderplank, who owned a fish and chip shop nearby, told the police that her Alsatian dog, Rex, barked several times for no apparent reason at the time that the robbers were later known to have arrived.

Perhaps the dog heard the gang cutting two iron bars on the rear window, and the breaking glass as they took out the window in order to gain entry. Inside, 3yds from the window, the thieves tackled the strongroom. They filled the keyhole with gelignite, held in place with modelling clay, then they ran an electric lead from the keyhole to an upstairs room and plugged it into a light socket. They exploded the gelignite by flicking the light switch. This led hairdresser Joseph Cretella, 59, who lived three doors away, to wake at around 1.00am, to the sound of what he thought was a car backfiring. He told police: "I went on to the balcony and looked out. I could see nothing so I went back to bed."

In the strongroom, a steel grille separated the thieves from the safe. They snipped off the grille's lock with bolt cutters, then gave the safe the gelignite treatment. From the safe they took £25,000 in notes, and from private deed boxes they took jewellery valued at £15,000. Police believed that at around 4.00am the gang used the bank's telephone to call their getaway car. The bank was an old building and had no burglar alarm, so the raid was not discovered until 6.30am, when the cleaner, Annie Lewis, arrived and as she passed the strongroom on the way to get her broom found tattered cushions and blankets strewn everywhere. Then she saw that the strongroom door was open, and dialled 999. The cushions and blankets, believed to have been used to muffle the explosions, were examined by Scotland Yard scientists.

Another daring raid was carried out at a bank in Kingston, Surrey, where a gang managed to escape with £46,000 in cash and jewellery. The only clues they left were a pair of gloves and a fragment of skin. One glove was found in the bank strongroom, which was blasted by gelignite after the gang had sawn through steel bars at the rear of the building. The other glove, said police: "came into their possession" later. The piece of human skin was found on glass on top of a wall over which the raiders had had to climb. Hospitals were asked to keep a lookout for anyone needing treatment for an injured hand.

The raiders had broken into Lloyds Bank on Clarence Street in Kingston. Bank raids had been on the increase for some time. Many of the buildings targeted were inadequately protected and, with the right tools and men for the job, robbing a bank was almost child's play. At this time, somewhere in Britain nearly every week, in the middle of the night there was a thud. A safe door would swing open and eager gloved hands would reach for the plunder. "That scene, played by several teams of the most expert safe-blowers ever known, has occurred almost weekly for the last two years," wrote a journalist in the *Mirror*. In that time, the "gelly" (gelignite) mobs had got away with more than £300,000 in hard cash and jewellery. Scotland Yard had had to appoint a special "Dragnet" squad to try and break the gangs. "Why are these gangs so successful?" asked the journalist. "Because they reduce the risk of capture to the lowest possible degree," he concluded. The raids were planned in meticulous detail, and seldom did a strike fail to produce a rich haul. It was clear that before the gangs made a big raid, they gathered inside information. The bank in Hounslow had been vulnerable, and the thieves knew they could enter the building from the rear. They also knew that a bolt cutter would break the guard bars. They knew they could operate from the back garden hidden from any patrolling policemen by a high wall. They also knew there was no burglar alarm. They knew exactly where the strongroom was, where the safe was situated, and they were pretty sure that on the night of the raid the safe would contain plenty of cash. Then came Kingston.

Police believed that one man controlled a number of "spotters", whose jobs were to identify potential premises. At this time, retail premises were just as likely to be the target as banks – especially when payday was imminent. It was understood that both men and women were involved. They would pick up scraps of information in pubs, clubs, trains and buses: police believed that in the course of a harmless conversation someone might let slip that he was paid on a Thursday. He may even mention the name of his firm. If the firm was a large institution, the spotter would then get to work finding out the number of employees and from which bank they would be paid; when the money was to be collected and where it was going to be put. If it was collected before payday and lodged in the firm's safe, the spotter would discover the position of the safe, what its strength was and how best the building could be accessed. Many of the places broken into were busy shops. It was here that police believed women were involved.

Posing as ordinary customers, the women observed as much as possible and tried to become friendly with an employee. According to the *Mirror*, it was child's play to discover in just a few short weeks, when the takings were banked and where they were kept overnight. After the preliminary spotting was complete, an experienced burglar "took sights", (looked over the shop) and made a note of local police activity. He also looked into the routines of neighbours and nearby shops. The burglar would then list the tools needed for the break-in. Police believed the cracksmen were young – they worked at great speed. It was also obvious that the raiders had a profound knowledge of explosives: they used just the right amount to blow the lock, but usually made no other damage. There was a good reason for this. Every safe had a secret packing of fibre, which could leave tell-tale clues on robbers' clothes. Seldom did the police find fingerprints – but they sometimes found glove smudges.

One important question was where did the gelignite come from? In the months before the end of 1957, there were repeated raids by thieves on explosive stores in the quarries on Dartmoor. In one raid, 488 sticks of explosive and an electric plunger (used for detonating) were stolen. Ten days later, 1,000 detonators vanished from another quarry. There was even a raid on a quarry at Dartmoor prison, although nothing was taken.

The gangs who blew open safes took elaborate precautions to avoid detection. The public was asked to help break them by noting strangers who seemed inquisitive about the firms they worked for, and viewing them with suspicion. Men or women standing aimlessly looking at busy shops or factories might be "spotters", the public was warned. People were told to report any heavy thuds they heard during the night. A 999 call would help police pinpoint targets, and with any luck allow them to find the perpetrators hard at work.

About a year after the bank raid in Kingston, Henry Preedy, 29, rued the day he moved to his new £3,500 house in Monks Drive, Acton. Nearby lived a Scotland Yard detective. On 6th November 1958, Preedy was jailed by the Old Bailey for four years for unlawfully possessing explosives. In the dock with him was 36-year-old John Rees, who admitted breaking into Lloyds Bank in Kingston. He was sentenced to 10 years in jail. If Preedy had not moved close to Flying Squad DI Bill Baldock's home (in Tudor Gardens), his association with Rees might never have led him into the dock.

Preedy hadn't actually taken part in the bank raid in which

gelignite was used, and Inspector Baldock probably wouldn't have noticed him. But Baldock's wife spotted the young man and the pretty young girl who moved into Monks Drive, and told her husband one night: "Whoever those people are, they seem to have plenty of money. All the furniture they moved in is new, and there's a brand new Armstrong Siddeley Sapphire car in the garage." The inspector didn't think much of it, as at the time he was busy trying to catch John Rees, wanted in connection with the Kingston bank raid. Then one morning, as he was setting off for Scotland Yard, he saw his new neighbour. Preedy's face registered with the detective immediately: he recognized the young man as having a criminal record, with nine convictions.

A month later, Inspector Baldock heard that bank raider Rees had been seen with a man named Preedy. From that moment, Baldock began to watch Preedy's house. One day, in August 1958, he saw Preedy leave the house in a Wolseley driven by another man. The driver, when the car returned, was Rees. He was seized by the detective and a colleague, and later the same day Preedy was also detained. In Preedy's house, the police found gelignite and detonators. While none of the money stolen in the Kingston raid was ever recovered, two other men were sent to prison for 10 years alongside Rees.

1958 – Bank Raids Become Big Business

By 1958, bank raids were gaining in notoriety and becoming much more sophisticated. However, smaller bank raids and one man bands were still in vogue. On 20th March that year, the 17-year-old son of an RAF air commodore appeared in court accused of bank robbery. Martin Searby, from the Hailsham area of Sussex, had stolen £2,274 from Lloyds Bank in Cranbrook, Kent. Searby was charged with robbery with violence, and appeared at Cranbrook court. His father, John, was in the USA at the time. The drama took place the day before, when the quiet little town of Cranbrook was settling down to an early closing day. A chauffeur-driven car drew up outside the bank, and a man got out.

Only the manager, Leonard Hopkins, and his staff of five were in the bank when a man wearing a raincoat and scarf entered the building. He asked to see Hopkins and was shown to his office. Seconds later, the rest of the bank staff saw Leonard Hopkins come out of his office. Behind him walked the man, apparently holding something a few inches from the manager's back. The raider ordered the staff to line up against a wall, then began to stuff a bag with bundles of notes. While he was doing this, a customer, Stanley Yeomans, 34, clerk of a local old people's home, walked in, and joined the line against the wall. As soon as the man left the bank, the manager raised the alarm. Every police car in the area was alerted and all roads were blocked. Twenty minutes later, in

Pembury, a car was stopped on a hill by two police cars that swung across the road. A man was taken to Cranbrook police station and detained.

When Searby was charged in court of robbing the bank at gunpoint, it was stated that he had "only just left school". A police inspector told Cranbrook magistrates that Martin Searby entered the bank at 1.00pm on the day in question and held up the manager and staff before leaving with the money. DS Deardon said that when Searby was charged he made a statement which amounted to an admission of the offence. He was granted legal aid at the request of his solicitor, Mr Bell. It was cited in court that the boy's parents did not wish to help in the matter. Searby was then remanded in custody. On 2nd April, Searby returned to court.

The bank manager had seen the getaway car's number plate – which by chance included his own initials and age. Immediately after the car left, he was able to give the number to police. In a statement Searby said: "I am sorry. I did a stupid thing. In my right mind, I would not have done it." The statement continued: "I would certainly not have used the gun." The prosecutor, Cooper, stated that Searby had picked up a hire car in Maidstone, and that the driver, Walter Turrell, was completely innocent. Searby, who had a suitcase and a holdall, told the driver to go to Lloyds Bank at Cranbrook and then on to London. Outside Lloyds, Searby said: "I won't be long." He took the holdall into the bank with him, then drew a .38 from his jacket and pointed it at Leonard Hopkins, who could see the gun was loaded. Searby said: "Don't do anything silly or I'll shoot." He took the money from the cashier's box and put it into the holdall, then returned to the car and apologized to Turrell for the delay, saying that he was in more of a hurry to get to London than he had been. The car was then stopped by the police in Pembury. PC Stace walked towards the vehicle, and Searby pointed the revolver at him before he tried to run away. Another police car approached, and PC Bradford chased Searby. When they were just a few feet apart, Searby warned the policeman to stop or he would shoot; but he then lowered the gun and allowed the policeman to arrest him. Later, the police found that the revolver was loaded and that Searby had 44 extra rounds of ammunition, a leather holster under his left arm, a picture of the bank and a knife in his possession. Searby was sent for trial and kept in custody. He pleaded not guilty and reserved his defence. The chairman of the magistrates commended PC Bradford on his calmness and bravery: "He has proved himself a great credit to the force."

"Make Believe Martin Gets 5 Years," read the headline in the *Mirror* on 5th July 1958. Reality hit for Martin Searby when it was announced in court that the young man lived in a world of make-believe. Before he was sentenced at Maidstone Assizes, the court was told of the fantasies – and the failures – in the life of this youth. At his public schools, Searby had been a failure. He was expelled from one of them for hiding cigarettes and alcohol. A year before the bank raid, he contacted the Russian Embassy in London and offered them documents which he thought were Bomber Command secrets – his father was Director of Bomber and Reconnaissance

Operations at the Air Ministry – which he then confessed to Scotland Yard. The documents were found to be valueless. Later, he tried to sell his father's camera so that he could "go to Israel to fight for the Jewish cause". Afterwards he enlisted in the Army, and immediately went absent; later, he bought himself out. But his "insane passion for notoriety" grew, the court was told. Searby went to Tangier to try and join an international smuggling ring, and rang up a £70 hotel bill – which he failed to pay. He was put in jail. Soon he went back home to Sussex and volunteered for the Parachute Regiment, but was rejected because of his flat feet. It was then that Searby concocted his most desperate plan yet: to rob the nearest bank to his old school in Cranbrook. The court was told how the driver of the car had no idea that the young man he had just picked up was about to rob a bank. Searby was known to have told a doctor that he did not feel "bound" by moral laws that were made before he was born. But the judge, Justice Cassels, passing sentence, said: "Although these rules were made before you were born, without the assistance of your wisdom they were made to bind you now that you are in this world." He added that he was sending Searby to prison because: "I don't take the view that Borstal, where you would have an audience and could pose as a real hero, is the place for you."

PC Victor Bradford, from Tunbridge Wells, was awarded the George Medal for his bravery in tackling the armed youth, even though he was threatened with the gun. He had grabbed Searby's wrist, forcing him to drop the loaded revolver.

In November 1958, Scotland Yard detectives believed that a mastermind criminal on the run from jail was the brain behind a £20,000 bank robbery committed on 31st October. Detectives thought that the man's escape from jail was organized by a gang who needed his expert knowledge: special equipment had been used to cut through the 9in thick "burglarproof" steel door to the bank's strongroom. The equipment – which included three giant oxygen cylinders and a new type of electrical cutting gear – was left behind by the raiders, and passed to Home Office experts for examination. While a widespread hunt got under way for the man and five others, the Midland Bank in London announced a £5,000 reward for information leading to the arrest and conviction of the raiders. A spokesman said: "We are not concerned with getting our money back. All we want is to get the people who did the job brought to justice." The raid was one of the best planned bank robberies of the time. To get to the strongroom in the basement of the Stoke Newington High Street branch, the gang worked for at least six hours during the night. They were believed to have driven a van carrying the heavy cutting equipment into a builder's yard at the back of the bank.

The iron bars of a basement window were cut with "Commando" clippers. One of the gang climbed through, and opened a back door to let the others in. The men then had to cut open an iron grille door before they could start cutting a hole in the steel door. When this was done, one of the raiders climbed into the strongroom and passed out the £20,000 – in bundles of £5, £1 and 10s notes. Most of the notes were old and the serial numbers were unknown. The raiders cleared the bank of all money except coins, having chosen a night when the bank was well stocked for Friday wage payouts.

On 2nd November 1958, a young London housewife, married for four years, was charged with breaking into the Midland Bank in Stoke Newington and stealing cash and jewellery, as well as receiving £8,727 belonging to the bank. The 22-year-old was Ada Margaret Shakeshaft, of Maida Vale, and she was to appear at North London magistrates the following day, having been detained for questioning the night before she was charged. Photographs of a man suspected of being one of the leaders of the raid were circulated to every police station in Britain, and officials at all ports and airports were also on the lookout for him. He beat a police swoop on a block of flats in Maida Vale only by seconds, and police found a large quantity of banknotes in the boot of a car parked near the property. Detectives, led by Detective Chief Superintendent Steve Glander, had gone to the flats to interview a 32-year-old man living on the top floor, but as they climbed the stairs, neighbours saw a man leave the flat and run down the back staircase. He left so quickly that when the detectives entered the empty flat an Elvis Presley record was still playing! The search continued in London for five other men who were believed to have taken part in the raid. The swoop that picked up Shakeshaft followed information given to Scotland Yard by an employee of a firm that made bolt cutters, who told the Yard that a man had asked for, and been sold, a pair of their most powerful cutters the week before. He became suspicious after reading about the raid.

While in custody, Shakeshaft said that it was more than her life was worth to tell police about her husband and his associates. She was charged at the magistrates' court with: "Being concerned with others in breaking and entering the Midland Bank in Stoke Newington High Street ... and stealing cash and jewellery worth £20,000, and ... receiving £8,727 in cash, knowing the money to be stolen." Ada Shakeshaft stood in the dock while Glander gave evidence. He said that late on the Saturday night, he saw Shakeshaft at the police station, where, after being told cash had been found in a locked vanity case at her home, she stated: "You can't hold me for that what my husband does. He has the money and was going off when the police called. I had the key, but he had one as well. He wouldn't let me have any of that money but told me to draw some from my bank until he got in touch with me. He didn't say where he was going, but I expect he will be with John and George. They are friends of Alan Bainbridge, I don't know their other names." Shakeshaft was then cautioned and asked if she wished to make a statement in writing. Her reply was: "It is more than my life is worth to say anything about them. I was never with them. Ken [her husband] was out all night on the Thursday you speak about. I went to Mr and Mrs Wooder's club at Westbourne Grove. I dare not say anything." When charged, Ada Shakeshaft denied she was guilty.

Another arrest followed on 7th November, and a club proprietor was charged in connection with the theft. Alan Bainbridge, 31, of

Wembley was arrested at his home and appeared before North London magistrates. He had been seen four days before arrest by detectives at Scotland Yard. They searched his club in Islington and his home. On 11th November, a detective admitted in court that the only evidence linking Ada Shakeshaft with the bank raid was the £8,727 in her vanity case. Richard du Cann, defending, asked the detective about the money which he confirmed had been found locked in the boot of a car near her home, and asked him to tell the court what actual evidence they had to link Shakeshaft with breaking and entering the bank. The detective was forced to reply that the police had no evidence at all. The court was then told that Ada Shakeshaft was not living with her husband at the time of the robbery, as marital relations had completely broken down. Du Cann applied for bail on his client's behalf, and offered to produce two sureties of £1,000 each, but this was refused, and the woman was once again remanded. However, she was granted bail on 17th November, despite police objections that she might "interfere" with their inquiries, including their search for her missing husband: Ken Shakeshaft had bolted before police could get to him. Bainbridge was also granted bail of £6,000, despite being known to have bought the two pairs of cutters used in the raid, from two Croydon firms. Ken Shakeshaft was also known to have bought a pair of bolt cutters from a firm on Euston Road – the man who sold them to him told the police the registration of his car.

Ada Shakeshaft was cleared of taking part in the bank raid on 24th November, but was still charged with receiving the cash. She was sent for trial. Alan Bainbridge was also sent for trial at the Old Bailey, accused of taking part in the robbery. He was jailed for four years in December 1958 for the help he gave to the gang. Before Bainbridge was sentenced, a police witness told the Old Bailey that the bank was robbed of £60,000, and not the £20,000 previously thought, the revised estimate coming from the fact that 50 strong boxes had been emptied. DS Harry Tappin added that the police thought most of the money was "well salted away". Judge Aarvold said that he got the impression that Bainbridge had some idea where the money had gone, but Bainbridge said nothing in court about it – nor about his exact part in the preparations for the raid. Neither did he talk about the gang leader, for whom he had obtained the steel cutting equipment. He was sentenced for being "an accessory before the fact" but not guilty of breaking and entering or stealing. Because of the equipment used, police knew that the mastermind behind the plan was an electrical specialist who had developed a new technique for cutting open strongrooms and safes.

November 1958 also saw the return of a maniac gunman who had shot and wounded a cashier at a bank while stealing £1,200 in August. On 12th November, the man walked into the same bank, the Brentford branch of the Midland Bank at Beecham House on the Great West Road, shot and wounded the manager and escaped with between £200 and £300. Police warned: "Take care – this man could be dangerous." Midland Bank again offered a £5,000 reward for information leading to the man's capture. It was just about closing time – 3.00pm – when the gunman swooped. Two female bank assistants and three cashiers were clearing up for the day, and the manager, Edward Aires, 52, was in his office. As the gunman entered, he pulled a purple and blue check muffler up to his face. After laying a blue canvas holdall on the counter, he drew out two revolvers and, pointing them at one of the cashiers, said: "I'm taking over now." The two women raced downstairs to the safety of the basement and the three cashiers dived underneath tables or through doors. One of them pressed the alarm bell as he dived for cover.

Hearing the bell, Edward Aires dashed out of his office. He had taken about six steps when the gunman turned and shot him in the stomach. As Aires fell, the gunman pushed him aside with his feet and leapt over the counter. On the other side, he came face to face with the cashier who was still pressing the alarm bell. For about 10 seconds the tense gunman pointed one of the guns straight between the cashier's eyes, while with his other hand he grabbed as many notes as he could, stuffing them into his pocket and the holdall. Then, quite calmly, he put his guns away and walked out. Meanwhile, the two female assistants had opened a window at the back of the bank and were shouting for help. A security officer, Stanley Wilkinson, 52, and another employee from Beecham House, Ernest Horne, rushed out of their offices. Wilkinson said: "As I pushed open the bank doors I found Mr Aires lying on his back on the customer side of the counter. He was still conscious and asked Wilkinson to get an ambulance. The last thing he said to the security officer was that he had seen the gunman and would know him again. Mr Aires was reported to be in a satisfactory condition in hospital. He had been the manager of the bank when the gunman had struck in August too. On that occasion, the man had held up the staff, shot down and wounded cashier Frank Lewis, 32, and got away with much more money. He was obviously not caught, and was therefore able to return in November. The two bank assistants told detectives that they were sure the raider was the same man. He was wearing a loose-fitting fawn or pale blue raincoat, with a scarf. Scotland Yard got their first clue regarding the movements of the gunman when a blue raincoat and hold-all were found on a train at Battersea station.

On 13th November, police staged a dramatic reconstruction of the four minutes in which the gunman shot down the bank manager in his second Midland Bank raid. The bank manager told the following story: "I was in my office when the gunman came into the bank. When the alarm bell sounded it was pressed by chief cashier, John Bennett, as he dived for cover. I opened my office door. I saw the gunman – but I didn't think he saw me and I dodged into my office to dial 999 and call the police. But my phone was not switched through to make an outside call. So, I went back into the bank and hid behind a pillar. The gunman was on the counter gathering up money and still did not realize I was there. So, thinking that I would be able to overpower him, I dodged behind a pillar. When he jumped down from the counter I rushed at him but failed to knock him over. As I did, he shot me in the stomach at point blank range. I fell to the floor but when he stepped over me, I put a foot out to trip him up. He stumbled but got to the door of the bank. Then he again threatened me with his guns." Police guarded the side of the bank as the doors were locked for the reconstruction. Two detectives played the parts of the bank manager and the gunman, while other members of staff took up the positions they were in when the gunman struck. The reconstruction was carried out three times, and all bank staff agreed that the raincoat and bag found at the station were those of the raider. Margaret Kirby, 24, told of her two ordeals with the same gunman – she'd seen his face twice – and was placed under police protection because she would be able to identify the man. He was described as being between 35 and 40 years old, and between 5ft 7in and 5ft 9in. He had black hair, which was straight and shiny with a parting on the right side. He had large eyes and a fresh ruddy complexion, and spoke with an Irish accent. The public were warned: "If you see this man, phone the police at once."

When Donald Brown, 39, was identified as the man that Scotland Yard wanted to interview in connection with the Brentford shooting, the police hunt went worldwide: on 23rd November 1958, Scotland Yard called in Interpol, the international police organization. Brown was known to have spent time in Paris and to have friends abroad. By the end of the month, 50,000 police in Britain had been issued with descriptions and pictures of him, while in London detectives swooped on West End clubs and restaurants, as the suspect was known to be fond of nightclubs. They also visited a number of houses in the Chelsea, Kensington and Shepherds Bush districts, as a result of a flood of telephone calls to the Yard from people claiming to have seen him. Meanwhile, the police guard on Margaret Kirby was strengthened; she had asked to be transferred to another branch of the bank, and her address was kept secret. The manhunt for Donald Brown was one of the largest carried out for years. Checks were made at railway stations, bus stations and long distance lorry depots all over the country. All civilian airports were warned to watch for him, as he was known to be able to fly small planes. The man they were seeking had changed his name by deed poll some months before the bank raids, and also used the alias John Lea or Lee. He was an electrician by trade and had, around the times of the raids, been working on a job in Welwyn Garden City in Hertfordshire.

By the end of the month, more than 600 possible clues as to Brown's whereabouts were being studied by police. A team of 12 detectives, led by Peter Sinclair, sifted through the reports, and from their headquarters in Brentford CID messages were sent out to police forces across the country, and further afield. Every item of information, including each anonymous tip off, was investigated. Brown had been seen with various women – for whom the police were also looking. Police in Northern Ireland and Eire were asked to keep a lookout for Brown, as were forces in the Channel Islands and France.

In February 1959, Margaret Kirby told journalist Peter Woods: "Now I shall be able to sleep at night without worrying." The young woman had been given the news that Donald (Brown) Hume was in police custody, charged with murder. "It is a great relief to me that it is all over." She had picked out the picture of Hume at Scotland Yard, thereby sparking a massive manhunt. Hume, an ex-Dartmoor prisoner, had been found in Switzerland – where his behaviour was baffling Swiss police. His chief interrogator, Police Commissioner Hans Stotz, told reporters that sometimes Hume burst into tears and shouted: "I killed a man. Go ahead – go on – hang me." At other times, he simply laughed at the questions he was asked. During one interview, Hume shaped two fingers like a gun, pointed to his own head and said: "Phut-Phut." Hume had been in a cell, and had undergone 30 hours of questioning.

Commissioner Stotz declared: "Sometimes during the questioning I feel very mad at him." Between his bouts of weeping and laughing, Hume was keeping a strange silence about 81 "lost" days in his life. This was the period between when he was believed to have escaped from Britain – where he was wanted for the two bank raids – and his capture after a Zurich hold-up, in which Hume shot and wounded a cashier and made off with about the equivalent of £18 in Swiss francs. He then shot dead a taxi driver – Arthur Maag, aged 50 – who tried to stop him. Stotz stated that Swiss and British police wanted to know what Hume had been doing since he left Britain. At his first interview with police, the strange man was given a cigarette which he tried to eat, and for two hours, he refused to admit he could speak English. He admitted to robbing the Swiss bank because he was broke. Stotz thought Hume was an extremely good actor. "In between questioning he has expressed a lot of regret about the killing of Maag." The penalty for murder in Switzerland was life imprisonment (25 years). Hume had been released from Dartmoor just 12 months earlier, having served eight years of a 12-year sentence for being an accessory to the murder of car dealer Stanley Setty. At his trial, Hume denied that he had anything to do with murdering Setty, but admitted that he had disposed of the body. After his release, however, he boasted that he had been responsible for the murder. After release, he changed his name by deed poll to Brown – the name under which he was charged with murder in Switzerland. Scotland Yard detectives wanted to learn from Hume just how he escaped from Britain. They believed that jailbreakers Alfred Hinds and Denis Stafford had left the country by the same method.

After his arrest, Hume had told the Swiss police that his name was John Stanislaw, and that he was an American citizen serving with the American Air Force at Wiesbaden in Germany. The questions facing police were: did John Stanislaw really exist, and if he wasn't just a fiction, was he still alive? They did not know what to think. However, they believed that Hume had arrived in Switzerland from Frankfurt in Germany, just before the raid. "He was wearing American service trousers, and he told us in questioning that he arrived at Zurich in a Lufthansa plane, with five American dollars in his pocket." A check established that there was no American serviceman named Stanislaw in Britain, but it was believed that Hume used the man's identify to leave Britain. American Service detectives continued their investigations into the putative John Stanislaw in Germany, but Hume stubbornly refused to give any more information. The 81 days were still unaccounted for.

As police built up their profile of Hume, they discovered more about him. He had been about to marry a beautiful Swiss divorcee named Trudi. Friends of the woman identified photos of Hume as the man they knew as her fiancé, Mr Bird. It transpired that Hume had been using a passport in the name of Stephen Bird, a British citizen, to travel in and out of Switzerland. One of Trudi's friends, Elizabeth Schunidthauser, said: "We have often seen this man this last May. He gave Trudi an engagement ring." Notice of the wedding had been given, she said, but the date had been postponed more than once – apparently because Bird had to go away on business. Clothes of Hume's found in Trudi's flat by police were removed for examination. Through Interpol, Scotland Yard were asked to try and find a man named Stephen Bird. The Yard believed that the real Stephen Bird was innocently trapped by Hume into revealing his birth date, and they suspected that he had never held a passport. They surmised that Hume had obtained a copy of the man's birth certificate from Somerset House – where all records were kept at that time – and applied for the passport; the men were the same age. The passport had been issued just a few weeks after Hume's release from Dartmoor, and it was suspected that Hume had been travelling in and out of Switzerland for months, being responsible for a number of hotel jewel robberies.

In February 1959, Hume admitted that he had raided the Midland

Bank in Brentford in November 1958, but he was not responsible for the robbery in August that year. However, the passport he was using showed that he had entered Switzerland immediately after both raids. He had also recently travelled to Canada, France, Germany and the USA. Meanwhile, it was revealed that Trudi Sommer had no connection with Hume's criminal history. "He seems to have used Switzerland as a jumping off place," the police said. There was also evidence, said Stotz, that Hume had disguised himself for some of his journeys abroad by growing a moustache and parting his hair in the middle. It was thought that Hume believed Switzerland had no police force, just a kind of fire brigade. Soon it was revealed that police in Germany were also interested in Hume: there had been three armed robberies in Frankfurt believed to have been carried out by a man answering his description.

Yvette Berube, the manager of a boarding house in Montreal, Canada, came forward to tell police that Hume had stayed there three times during 1958 under the name of John S Bird. She had discouraged his unwanted advances. He had stayed there in August, October and December – the last time for three weeks. He had left his suitcases with her, and had promised to return for them after Christmas 1958. By this time, police were looking into crimes committed in Montreal at the time of his visits.

Hume was then examined by police psychiatrists in April 1959. A mind examination was part of the Swiss legal procedure in all major criminal cases. It was expected to last two months; his trial was not scheduled for another four or five months.

Bank Raids

Hume eventually stood trial in September, being known in court as Donald Brown. For Tom Tullett, writing in the *Mirror*, Hume was a vain man whom he had met shortly after his release from Dartmoor. Tullett described the defendant as an egotist who liked to boast about his time in prison, where apparently he had things "well organized". When he met Tullett in a pub in Fleet Street – journalist territory – Hume was "delighted" when people in the bar recognized him. When asked how he felt about the detectives who had arrested him over the Setty murder, his face was "distorted with hate". He recovered in just a moment, and told Tullett that all he wanted to do was start a new life abroad. He talked about Dartmoor, and how he had hidden a revolver in a wireless set for a man who planned to escape. He talked about how he had the run of the prison as a "trusty"; he was given extra food and drink was brought in for him. Tullett concluded: "This man is one of the vainest I have ever met."

During the Second World War, Hume had joined the RAF and had called himself Terence. He loved wearing the uniform: it suited his ego. He became interested in women. At the time, he wrote: "Yesterday I was jilted for once, by a cinema girl. Bah Jove. I nearly went mad. You should have seen the letter I wrote her, and I also turned all the other lads against her by a little vicious propaganda ..." In 1939, he went to hospital with cerebro-spinal meningitis. When he recovered, he was classed as unfit for flying, and was discharged from the RAF. He got a job as a fitter with an aircraft firm, but he wanted more glamour. In 1942, Hume bought two uniforms from an ex-RAF officer, stole an RAF identity card and was next seen wearing the uniform of a sergeant pilot. He visited a firm in Twickenham where he had worked and was given a hero's welcome – and a director gave him £10. In uniform, Hume found it easy to gain money. He cashed cheques all over London, and thus began a career in crime.

Hume was eventually arrested for masquerading as an officer, and was sent to Feltham prison for medical treatment. Later, he was bound over. He then promoted two companies, made money, and married – but he also loved the nightlife of London's West End. Then he killed Setty. The years in jail did little to change him, except to make him more determined to make money. At this time he changed his name to Brown. When Hume came to trial in September, charged with the murder of Arthur Maag and robbing a Zurich bank, he repeatedly insulted the judge. He was led into the crowded court at Winterthur with chains linking his wrists to his ankles, two policemen with Tommy guns following him. He created sensation after sensation, telling the distinguished judge, Dr Hans Gut, 50, to "get lost". In a jaunty, arrogant mood, Hume referred to the judge as "buster" and "old feller", and at one point called him an "old bum". He even threatened to "tear him to bits" both physically and verbally. With an amazing calm, Hume admitted in court that he was responsible for the two bank raids and shootings in Brentford, as well as the bank raid in Zurich. Hume's confession about the Midland Bank robberies came as he was being questioned about his past. He said he was armed during the raids because he felt "lonely". He described in court how he had planned both Midland Bank raids "like a war operation", and that he had bought a second pistol in Bern before returning to London in early November 1958. The reason he had returned to the same branch of the bank was that during the first raid the staff had outwitted him. When he had asked them to open the big safe, they had replied that there was nothing in it but books and papers. He said: "I just felt I had to go back. I don't like people putting anything over on me." The second raid was purely revenge. Hume told the court that he had no qualms or regrets about what had happened at the two bank raids in Brentford, but he did "give a damn" about what happened in Zurich. Then he stunned the court by admitting that he had murdered car dealer Stanley Setty, whose dismembered body had been found in the Essex marshes in 1949. He described how he had fought with Setty and killed him with a knife, later putting the man's head in a parcel, his body and arms in another and his legs in a third package. He then threw them from a private plane. In court, Hume clearly displayed three different sides of his personality: the hesitant, the romantic and the braggart.

Hume's hesitation on the brink of crime was revealed on the second day of the trial, when he said that he had been trying to pluck up enough courage to raid the Zurich bank. He had wandered the city the day before, feeding swans on the lake before spending a sleepless night in the English church. He had done a great deal of thinking and realized that he couldn't build a paradise with a gun. But the other side of his personality told him not to be a coward. He said that he knew the raid would fail. He talked about Trudi Sommer and how he had tried to forget her, but couldn't. He confirmed that she knew nothing about his criminal activities. It was only when a map of the Zurich bank was produced that Hume began to brag. He swaggered across the courtroom, and pointed out that given his position when he shot the chief cashier, Walter Schenkel, he could not have intended to kill him. When it came to the second shooting in Brentford, Hume said: "The English bank manager threw himself on me." He added: "In England there is a death penalty for murder. But they ought to have a law to stop bank managers from attacking people – after all, I was the injured party." In court, Hume "made eyes" at Yvonne Maag, not knowing that she was the daughter of the man he shot dead. Banking apprentice Ulrich Fitze, 16, told the court that Arthur Maag had been shot as he chased Hume through the streets. Hume had shot the taxi driver from around 30ft when Fitze called out to Maag to stop him. In the closing speeches, the Swiss Public Prosecutor, Dr Paul Lienhart, remarked that a "Farcical English law taught Donald Hume that crime does pay". He described the failings of the British judicial system – pointing out that Hume could not be tried twice for the murder of Setty. He also condemned the British legal system for allowing a criminal like Hume four years remission on his 12-year sentence; in his view the defendant should have stayed inside. He asked the jury to find Hume guilty on all three counts of murder, attempted murder and robbery. A Zurich psychiatrist told the court that the prisoner was psychopathic, unfeeling, vain and sexually insatiable.

On 1st October 1959, 10 years after the murder of Setty and

almost a year since the second Brentford bank raid, Hume was sentenced to life imprisonment. He was found guilty on all three counts. The Swiss authorities were determined that Hume would never go free again.

The 10 people who helped to capture Hume shared the £6,000 reward offered by Midland Bank. Those who benefited from the largest portions were Fitze, and Gustav Angstmann – who had tackled Hume after the bank raid in Zurich and taken his gun from him. The remainder of the money went to Arthur Maag's family.

Hume's condition deteriorated in jail, and he became so violent two years into his sentence that a special strongroom cell was built for him. He tore his bed apart, making two "swords" from the steel in the frame. His shouting and screaming brought warders to the cell door, which they found barricaded. Hume shouted for two packets of English cigarettes, and when he didn't get them he became wilder still. It was decided that he was so dangerous that he would have to be quelled with teargas.

Hume wrote to Scotland Yard in August 1965, in connection with the inquiry into whether Timothy Evans was responsible for the murder of his baby daughter. Hume wrote that Evans had admitted to him 15 years earlier while they were in Brixton jail together that he had killed the infant, because of her constant crying. The inquiry was looking into whether Evans was properly convicted and hanged for the murder. He had lived at 10 Rillington Place in Notting Hill with John Christie, who had been hanged three years after Evans for murdering eight women, including Mrs Evans.

Hume was eventually brought back to Britain in 1976, and sent to Broadmoor. He was returned in chains after Swiss officials and the Home Office decided he was an extremely dangerous man: the Swiss wanted rid of him because his mental condition was steadily deteriorating. Once Hume arrived, he was examined by two doctors, who immediately signed an order for him to go to Broadmoor.

1959 – Girl Bandit Hunted by Scotland Yard, and Raids Increase

The month before Scotland Yard mounted a hunt for a female bank robber wanted in connection with £20,000 stolen from Midland Bank, a three-year-old spaniel named Twinkle foiled a similar robbery, on 14th June 1959. Charles Johnson, 37, returned home late from a party with his wife, and they let Twinkle out onto the veranda at the back of their first-floor flat on the Old Kent Road, in Camberwell. The dog barked, and Johnson went out to see what she was barking at. He saw men at the back windows of the bank, close to the flat, and immediately dialled 999. The raiders had removed half a window frame and had cut away a protecting iron grille at the Old Kent Road branch of the Midland Bank.

When Twinkle barked, the raiders fled, leaving oxyacetylene cutting equipment inside the bank – having failed to reach the £10,000 in the bank's strongroom. (Oxyacetylene was used by welders to produce an intensely hot flame.) Police cordoned off the area and later detained four men. A bank official told the *Mirror* that banks were not ungenerous at times like this – meaning that they had offered a reward.

In July that same year, a slim girl was hunted by detectives who were investigating the large haul taken from another branch of the

Midland Bank in London – this time in Mile End Road, Stepney. Described in the press as the "moll", the woman was described as fair-haired and part of a London gelignite gang. It was believed that she had opened the way for male accomplices who had cracked a safe. Police were working on the theory that the woman had sat in the Empire cinema, next to the bank, just before the cinema closed, then hid in a toilet. Later, she crawled out onto a flat roof and let herself down with a rope into the bank's backyard. There, it was thought she used a car jack to force apart two iron bars at a window. They were parted by just a foot – enough for a slim girl to slip through, break a windowpane and get in. Once inside, she forced an outer door from the inside, before climbing back into the cinema, opening an emergency door and letting in the rest of the gang, who were waiting in a deserted passage with their equipment.

A third raid was carried out on another Midland Bank brand on Seven Sisters Road, Finsbury. Here, around £2,000 was stolen by a gelignite gang. A fourth raid was carried out by possibly the same gang at another branch in Ilford, Essex, but was a disaster for the raiders when they blew the wrong steel door and only found documents. In other raids, £11,000 was stolen from the American Express tourist offices in Mayfair, and £4,300 was grabbed from an ice-cream factory in Stonebridge Park, Middlesex.

In August 1959, Dennis Cashman took up his newly appointed position as a special weekend security patroller. The 33-year-old set out on 2nd August to visit six London branches of Midland Bank as part of the bank's latest plan to beat the weekend raiders. At the first five branches all was well. But as Cashman stepped into the sixth – at Commercial Street in Stepney – he heard scuffling noises from the vaults. He went downstairs to investigate, and found a gang of thieves working in the gloom to break open the main vault's safe, in which there was £30,000. He ran back upstairs and immediately called the police. Almost at once, the bank was surrounded by police and their dogs. The raiders, however, had fled empty-handed through a hole they had made in the bank wall, and through the side door of a greengrocer's warehouse next door. In the rush to escape, they left their gear, including an oxyacetylene cylinder and elaborate electrical cutting equipment. The raiders, who were thought to have got into the bank by way of the warehouse late on the Saturday night, also left a bottle of whisky, bottles of beer, flasks of tea and sandwiches. Cashman said: "When the police arrived, the iron grille leading to the vaults was still warm from the acetylene cutter the gang used to get through it." He continued: "This was my first day on security patrol. I volunteered for the extra duty ... in the week I work at the Midland's head office." He described how everything in the sixth branch had seemed all right before he heard noises from the basement. He thought that nobody outside the bank would have noticed, or heard, anything odd, and he didn't think that once the gang went back into the street from the warehouse they would have been noticed, as there were already quite a few people around. The raid was one of a growing number on Midland Bank targets: in another, a gang were disturbed as they tried to rob the Midland Bank in Upton Park.

In November 1959, police throughout London were ordered by Scotland Yard to keep a "day-and-night watch" for the woman that the underworld called the "Jelly Babe". Detectives hoped that catching her would hand them the key to rounding up a gang of safe-blowers who were raiding banks with the use of gelignite (or jelly, as it was nicknamed). They knew the woman worked with the gang (which had managed to scoop more than £100,000 in six months), and they knew that she was present during the raids because someone was slim enough to crawl through holes in strongroom walls. Four times in 1959, detectives investigating bank raids and other safe-blowing robberies in London had found clues that indicated a woman was working with the gang. In the first case, a woman's size four shoe was found at the scene. The second clue was found at Westminster Bank in Chingford, Essex, where an attempt had been made to blow the safe. The hole was just about big enough for a slim woman to wriggle through. The third clue was an imprint of a woman's size four shoe that was left at a burgled office in Mayfair, and the final one was a hole blown through the strongroom wall at a branch of the National Provincial Bank in Chingford, Essex, again just big enough for a woman to crawl through. On this last occasion £16,000 was taken. The police had also become aware that the Jelly Babe was an expert driver; she had got away from the Flying Squad cars that had been detailed to tail her.

In December 1959, a police constable, a mother, her daughter and son and two other men were charged in connection with the National Provincial raid at Chingford. Earlier, in raids on a number of houses, a squad of 40 detectives took possession of £2,000 and some jewellery. Late on 8th December, Scotland Yard announced that the four men, charged with breaking and entering, and stealing cash and jewellery, were PC George Askew, 39, of the Metropolitan Police, John Young, 71, from Harringay, William Goodwin, 30, from Essex, and Edward Irving, 34, from Tottenham. All four were remanded in custody. The two women, who were charged with receiving money and jewellery, were Rose Irving, 57, and her daughter, Beryl Irving, 24; they were both granted bail. The men were kept on remand. DCI Henry Baker told Waltham Abbey magistrates that "a vast amount of the money has not been recovered and has to be traced". He felt that three of the men would abscond if given bail.

PC Askew appeared on remand at Chingford alongside the other accused men, where it was stated that he had told police that at the time of the raid he was having dinner with a solicitor and an MP. However, PC Askew's statement about the dinner was challenged in the magistrates' court, where he appeared again on 22nd December. The policeman denied that he had ever made a statement to that effect while in police custody. John Young, in the meantime, told magistrates that they should be looking for a man named Humphreys.

Police had tailed PC Askew for nearly a month, being watched almost daily by a team of detectives. He was charged with three counts of breaking and entering as well as stealing cash and jewellery. When his house was searched, £1,559 10s was found, together with traces of gelignite in the hip pocket of a pair of his trousers. This was a perfect match for the gelignite found at a recent laundry break-in. Askew had been on the beat at the time of the break-in at the Westminster Bank, a job he had asked for. He claimed to have discovered the break-in at about 5.30am, and called for assistance. When a colleague arrived, he told him that the bank had been robbed, and that the thieves must have got in by cutting through the window bars. At this time, Askew was outside the wire fence at the back of the bank, from where there was no sign of a break-in. When police arrived at the laundry break-in, they had discovered Askew hiding in a doorway in his uniform. The raiders on that occasion had been disturbed and nothing was stolen, but police were confident that Askew had been present before the alarms went off, alerting police.

Askew was sent for trial on 18th January 1960, together with Irving, Young and Goodwin. Regarded by his seniors as a quiet, plodding policeman, honest and unspectacular, Askew was found guilty and given seven years in jail. Far from being the honest, quiet PC that his colleagues and superiors had thought, Askew was in fact the key member of a daring gang of bank raiders. His life of crime and his 10-year career in London's police ended after the trial, which lasted 21 days. The three other men were found guilty as well. Irving and Goodwin were also given seven years, while Young was sentenced to five years. Irving's mother was found not guilty of receiving stolen property.

Askew had developed a taste for luxury living and expensive clothes while serving with the Palestine police during the Second World War. It led to him becoming a crooked cop, a man on the beat who knew the times of police patrols and the whereabouts of radio cars. He was a man who always knew the best place – and the safest time – to strike. He had met Irving and Goodwin not long after he was posted to Chingford in 1956. Askew told his police colleagues that his hobby was betting on horses, and he often spoke of the money he had won so that no one would wonder how a £13-a-week policeman managed to afford regular visits to West End nightclubs. Askew came under suspicion soon after the National Provincial raid, when he bought a new car and paid a £1,500 deposit on a bungalow. CID men investigated, and found the cash at his house as well as traces of gelignite. There was still no sign of the Jelly Babe.

1960 – Warning From the Lord Chief Justice to Bank Bandits Goes Unheeded

Lord Parker, the Lord Chief Justice, told a bank bandit in the Appeal Court in November 1960 that he would not reduce his seven-year sentence, even by one day. "Raids on banks have got to stop," said Lord Parker. The court dismissed the appeal of Edward Irving. John Young also lost an appeal.

It seemed, though, that the warning went unheeded. In September 1960, bank raiders were believed to have used the M1 motorway before and after claiming a haul of £25,000. After a raid in Birmingham, Scotland Yard asked a number of suspects in London's underworld, at the request of Birmingham detectives, to account for every hour of their movements over the previous weekend. Yard detectives realized that the raid could have been clinched in less than seven hours, including the 220-mile trip from London to Birmingham and back, part of which they suspected was carried out at high speed on the M1.

The raid took place at Barclays Bank in Bordesley High Street. Inside the bank's strongroom, the gang forced open a safe and scooped up the contents, which was in £1 and £5 notes. A senior Birmingham detective said: "The raid bears the stamp of a London gang who are suspected of previous safe raids in the

Bank Raids

Midlands." Police believed that at least one gang member lived in the Birmingham area, and had tipped off the Londoners about suitable premises. It was thought that the raiders arrived in their own car, carrying pickaxes and tools. It would have only taken two suitcases to remove the £25,000. However, their celebrations were short lived.

On 15th December 1960, James Hulme Milne, 28, whom detectives had nicknamed "Prince of the Peter Boys" (safe-breakers), was sentenced to 10 years imprisonment for robbing the bank of £27,000. "Prince" stood motionless in the dock at Birmingham Assizes as Mr Justice Paull addressed him: "You played for high stakes. People like you who take part in these so carefully planned and well-executed robberies for large sums of money must realize they do so at the peril of going to prison for a very long time." Milne paused in the dock just long enough to fold his expensive raglan overcoat over his arm, then strolled casually down to the cells below to start his sentence. It took the jury just eight minutes to find the Birmingham man guilty of breaking into Barclays Bank, and stealing cash and jewellery. They heard how Milne and other men tunnelled through the back wall of the bank during the quiet of a September weekend, then broke into the strongroom. Afterwards he went on a spending spree to Scotland, buying a new car, TV, tape recorder and other luxuries, and opening two bank accounts. But seven weeks after the raid, he was trapped after an accident.

While driving his new car, Milne was hurt in a crash, and was taken to Birmingham's Queen Elizabeth Hospital. As he was undressed by nurses, so X-rays could be taken, thick wads of notes tumbled from his pocket. The nurses, who were suspicious, called the police, and they discovered that the serial numbers matched those of the stolen money. In a statement, Milne had admitted that his share of the haul was £6,500, but in court he said this statement was untrue; that at the time he made it, he had been suffering from concussion. He claimed that the money had come from wins on the horses. But Milne had a record. He had been to Borstal for safe-breaking, prison for safe-breaking and had been discharged from the Army for his "psychopathic personality".

While serving his three-year sentence for safe-blowing (and stealing £2,100), Milne wrote a one-act play for television. Later he appeared in a documentary about the rehabilitation of ex-criminals, and announced: "I am reformed." But there was still £19,000 missing from the bank haul, and police knew that at least three other men were involved in the raid. Milne, however, was keeping quiet.

In September 1963, it was announced that Milne was being sued by the bank he had robbed, because it was found that he had £4,000 in two accounts. The bank claimed the money as part of the robber's proceeds. Milne, who was serving his sentence in Pentonville prison, conducted his own defence, and argued that the court had no power to touch the money in his accounts, also claiming that he had nothing to do with the robbery and that the £4,000 came "from normal profits of business". However, Milne lost his nest egg after a High Court judge in London ordered that it should be returned to Barclays Bank. Milne refused to transfer the money, and the National Commercial Bank of Scotland, in which he had £3,000, decided that they didn't have the right to transfer their client's money without his instructions.

A month before Milne was sentenced to 10 years in prison, bandits who broke into Barclays in Queensway, Bayswater, got away with £100,000. However, police revealed that a single penny might just trap them. This penny was found on the floor near the bank's two strongrooms, and police thought it was a coin flipped to see which of the two rooms to open. There were a thumbprint and part of a fingerprint on it. The strongroom which they broke into had yielded a haul of £25,000 cash and an estimated £75,000 in jewels and silver from deed boxes; the other only held papers and ledgers. The bank raiders had struck during a weekend, having learned that a flat directly above the bank had become vacant on a Friday: the woman who had occupied it for 15 years had made it widely known that she was moving. On the Saturday, the raiders walked through a door that led from the street to four flats over the bank. They broke into the empty flat and cut a hole in the floor, then another in the ceiling of the bank. Through the holes went five 2cwt cylinders of oxyacetylene. The raiders carried the cylinders down six steps to the strongrooms, and after they had cut a hole in the strongroom door, one raider crawled through. He handed out the cash and deed boxes, then with small iron bars the gang forced open the deed boxes, and rifled them before leaving.

A dressmaker who worked near the bank saw two young men

and a girl get out of an American car and take suitcases up to the flat over the bank. Later she observed men carrying cylinders, but she assumed they were from the water board. On the Saturday night, she heard a steady buzzing noise, like a drill. It having been decided that the basement and side walls of the bank were not strong enough, workmen had been strengthening the walls from the inside for a fortnight, and dust sheets that they had left were used by the bandits to mask their torch lights and flames.

That same month, Flying Squad cars and police from all over London were diverted to Chiswick in the search for an 18-year-old girl and her tattooed boyfriend, whom they wanted to interview in connection with a Sussex bank raid. The hunt moved from Sussex to Chiswick after a Portsmouth taxi driver told police that this was where he had dropped a couple who answered descriptions of the pair. Geoffrey Halstead had driven the couple around all day, from Portsmouth to Southampton, then to Salisbury, before heading for London: a seven-hour journey. The cab fare cost the couple £15, which they paid for in £5 notes.

The girl, Valerie Joan Salter, had vanished from her home in Worthing. Her boyfriend, Victor John Terry, 20, was from Chiswick, and had four words tattooed on his right arm: Maureen, Mabel, Vic and Knife. The driver had dropped the couple in the Acton/ Ealing area, not far from Chiswick, and squad cars ringed Terry's home. Uniformed police and detectives searched the neon-lit cafés and pubs in Chiswick High Road, and at midnight, 60 detectives with three police dogs cordoned off Devonshire Road having been

Bank Raids

informed that Terry was in the area. Police went from house to house, trying doors and looking in basements as well as checking back gardens. Lights burned in Terry's council flat. Both sets of parents appealed for Salter and Terry to come home.

In a special court on 12th November 1960, a 16-year-old boy and a 20-year-old youth, Alan Hosier, were jointly accused of the murder of John Henry Pull, 61, a bank guard who was shot dead at the Durrington, Sussex, branch of Lloyds Bank. The police found the body of Pull in the bank and quickly found the two accused. The boy was named in court, but as he was still a juvenile he was not named in the press at this point. The accused were both remanded.

More than 68,000 policemen were searching for the couple, and after a nationwide search they were arrested in Glasgow. At one o'clock in the morning, a detective knocked softly on the yellow door of room 12 at the Lynedoch Hotel. Most of the guests in the 15-roomed hotel were in bed. DI Hector McDougall's knock was answered, and the couple were asked to dress. Within a few minutes they were driven away in two cars to a city police station, where Terry was charged with the murder of John Pull (alongside the two others), and Salter was charged with receiving stolen money. Police in Worthing were notified of the arrests. Scotland Yard's Bob Acott and Alfred Rudd, called in by Sussex police to help with the murder, had just gone to bed in their Worthing hotel: it was the first time they had been able to get some sleep in more than 76 hours. Immediately they rushed back to the station. Two magistrates were woken and asked to sign two warrants, necessary under Scottish law, to bring the couple back to England. Chief of West Sussex CID Alan Hoare and Sgt Nora Thomson were also called from their beds. The police were taken by helicopter from Shoreham to London Airport. When Salter and Terry arrived, they were driven in separate cars to Worthing.

The couple had arrived at the Glasgow hotel from London at 8.00am in the morning. The hotel owner, Eunice Walker, said the couple looked tired, and Terry asked for a double room. He said they were married, and paid for two days in advance. The couple went out soon after arriving and came back at around 2.00pm, leaving again shortly afterwards. Walker had read about Terry and Salter, and was suspicious that they could be the couple in her hotel. She phoned a cousin to talk through her suspicions, but was still unconvinced. Just after 6.00pm the fugitives returned, and they were shown to the TV lounge where they watched *Juke Box Jury*. They went to bed just before 11.00pm, but Eunice Walker stayed and watched the news, during which a photo of Salter was flashed on the screen. She immediately recognized the girl and phoned her cousin again, who came round in his car. At midnight they went to the Glasgow Marine police station, and told police of their suspicions. The couple went quietly when they were arrested.

Terry and Salter appeared separately before magistrates in Worthing on 14th November 1960. Both were remanded in custody and respectively driven to Brixton and Holloway prisons in London. Their departure was watched by a crowd of more than 300. The prosecution hearing against the three youths who were accused of murdering John Pull opened in early December. Just before it began, Valerie Salter was charged with being an accessory to the murder. Bank cashier Andrew Barker, 21, told the court on 8th December 1960 of the "sheer terror" that gripped him when he saw bank guard John Pull shot dead. It was terror, he added, that prompted him to call after one of the raiders who grabbed an empty bag after the shooting. "Not that one," he called. The raider returned, threw the empty bag to the ground and sized another, containing £1,372. Two raiders then ran out. By this time, 16-year-old Philip Tucker had been named in the press. The prosecution alleged that Tucker had entered the bank with Terry, and that the older youth fired point blank at Mr Pull after he raised his hand as if to speak. Hosier was alleged to have waited outside the bank in a stolen car. Salter was also in the dock that day, accused of being an accessory after the fact of murder and receiving stolen money. Barker told the court how he and Pull had arrived at the sub-branch of Lloyds Bank shortly before 10.00am with a bag of money, which was attached to Mr Pull by a chain. When they reached the bank, the bag was unchained and put on the counter, where there was another bag. A minute after 10.00 am, a customer entered the bank. Barker dealt with her for a few seconds, then Mr Pull went to the cloakroom. Shortly afterwards, two men entered the bank and walked casually along the passage that led to the back of the office. Barker challenged the men as they walked past him, but they reached the back office at about the time John Pull was coming out of the cloakroom with a kettle in his hand. One of the raiders, Terry, was standing close to the safe; the other was positioned nearer the passage. Then Terry levelled a gun at Pull, who was completely taken by surprise. For several seconds, both Barker and Pull just stared at the two thieves. Then Pull raised his arm (it was something he always did before speaking), and touched Terry on the arm. Terry drew away, and fired. John Pull fell face down, and both men then turned towards Andrew Barker. He identified Terry as the man with the gun, but he thought it was Hosier in the bank with him, not Tucker. After the men had gone, Barker went to the door and caught sight of a bottle-green saloon car going towards Goring, then ran from the front door to the back and called the police, also setting off the alarm bell. Then he ran outside and asked a man standing by a wall to come in. This was Maurice Taylor, a greengrocer. When he entered the bank he saw Mr Pull lying face down in a pool of blood, with another member of the public trying to help him. Taylor pulled the dying man into his arms and stayed with him. He was unconscious but making a faint noise – a rattle was coming from his chest. Pull died before the doctor arrived, and Maurice Taylor gently laid him down. Shortly afterwards the police arrived.

It transpired in court that there was a striking resemblance between Hosier and Tucker, and also that the taxi in which Salter and Terry had travelled from Portsmouth to Southampton and Wiltshire before heading for London had been stopped three times. On none of these occasions did police recognize the couple in the back as the fugitives they were seeking. Part of the evidence was a coat, belonging to Terry, which had been found in Salter's mother's home. In the pocket were a rifle bolt, cartridge extractor and 14 cartridges. There were also six small spots of blood on the coat, believed to come from John Pull.

The trial of the four accused began on 20th March 1961 at Lewes, but all denied the charges against them. Terry was under a strange delusion at the time he staged the hold-up, the court was told. He believed that his mind and body had been "invaded" by the spirit of the American gangster Legs Diamond. So elaborate was the delusion that Alan King-Hamilton QC, defending Terry on the charge of capital murder, told the court that when he drove away with Salter it wasn't him at all but Legs Diamond and his gangster moll. He didn't dispute the fact that Terry was there and had organized the raid, but said that his client firmly believed he was not the one in control. The court was therefore informed that Terry's main defence was "diminished responsibility". His defence counsel told the court that he planned to provide evidence to show that Terry was in "no man's land" at the time of the shooting and robbery.

Terry had become subject to moods, hallucinations and delusions as a teenager, sometimes consistent with schizophrenia. He often heard voices telling him what to do, but instead of seeking medical assistance he sought a supernatural explanation. Terry believed that the spirits of dead people invaded the bodies of the living, and was convinced that some of those spirits had occupied him. He had been afraid to tell anyone of the delusions, in case they laughed at him; and on top of this he became a drug addict. A month before the bank raid, Terry was fired from his eleventh job in

Worthing. His employers were convinced he had been taking a drug known as Purple Heart.

On 23rd March 1961, a psychiatrist told of the "dream world" in which Terry was living: he believed he was an agent of another planet who might "take over the whole world" one day. Dr Arthur Paterson said that he had come to the conclusion that the man was not responsible for his actions, and was a case of diminished responsibility. He said that Terry suffered from schizophrenia, and had tried to see a psychiatrist after telling his parents he would shoot somebody. He had been well aware that he would probably end up accused of murder, and wanted to be a great gangster. He had even had thoughts of harming his mother with a knife. Terry told the doctor that when he had these thoughts he did not feel as if he was himself, or in control of his own body. He also told the doctor he thought he was an enemy from another planet. Dr Paterson, under cross-examination, said that at the time of the raid Terry was insane, in the medical sense. But he added that Terry knew that what he was doing was wrong, and agreed that he was not insane in a legal sense. Paterson went on to say that he believed Terry lived more in his dream world than he did in reality. Matilda Terry, the accused's mother, also told the court that her son had admitted to "strange feelings"; that he had told her there was something or someone stronger than him in his body.

However, another psychiatrist, Dr John Wyndham Pearce, said that Terry's possessed mind was entirely fictitious. He had been called by the prosecution to rebut the two other psychiatrists' evidence. He found no abnormality in Terry, and when the young man told him of Legs Diamond invading his body the doctor had feigned ignorance, forcing Terry to talk about the 1930s gangster. He also talked to the doctor about the drugs he had been taking. The doctor thought that Terry was very careful to observe his reactions, and the extent to which he was accepting what was being said. Paterson added that Terry told him he had a mania for guns; that Terry had been made a fool of by his peers; that he had originally loved animals, but had taken to hurting them: he said he "[drove] ... everything into the ground with my boot". At this point, he flushed slightly, and the doctor told the court that he was acting like an actor warming up for his time on stage. The doctor concluded that everything that Terry said was play-acting. The judge, Mr Justice Stable, 73, agreed, and told counsel for Terry that there was "not a particle of evidence" to show that the accused was suffering from a mental disease caused by taking drugs, or otherwise, when he murdered John Pull. Defence counsel had asked the jury to say that Terry was suffering from diminished responsibility, and to find him guilty of manslaughter, rather than murder, but the judge directed them otherwise. The case was brought to an end on 28th March 1961, it having taken the jury 163 minutes to find all four guilty. The judge sentenced Victor Terry to death for the murder of John Pull. Alan Hosier was found guilty of non-capital murder and sentenced to life imprisonment. Philip Tucker was found guilty of non-capital murder and ordered to be detained. The judge gave permission for the parents of Hosier and Tucker to see their sons in the cells. Mr Justice Stable then turned his attention to Valerie Salter, who was found guilty of being an accessory after the fact and put on probation for a year. The judge said: "If ever a human being was put in an appalling dilemma as to what they ought to do, you were. As a judge, I am bound to tell you that you had no business to do anything to assist the chap to whom you had given your heart to escape. As a human being, I am not at all sure. I am satisfied with this: that you did what you believed to be right, and if people do what they really believe to be right they cannot do very much wrong. Now, my dear, at your very young age you have been faced with the most awful tragedy. You have obviously given your heart to this man. I suppose there is nothing sadder than to see the things one believed in, and perhaps loved, shattered. That is what breaks people's hearts. Your heart is a very young one. Do not imagine today it is broken. I expect it hurts – but it will mend ... Go back to your family and start afresh." Mr Justice Stable was in tears as he walked to his car from the courtroom in Lewes Assizes: he had left behind three young men whom he had sentenced for the murder of John Pull and one sobbing teenager.

In the dock, Terry stood with his feet apart, gripping the rails. He remained motionless as the judge put the black cap on his head, but swayed when the judge passed the death sentence. He was then taken to the cells below. The judge had not thought it a good idea for Valerie to be allowed to see Terry after the trial ended, but his parents were allowed to see him in a large cell. Meanwhile, it was reported that two people were considered eligible to claim the

£10,000 reward in connection with the case. They were Eunice Walker and Matthew Wilson, a Worthing taxi driver who had been suspicious of two of the accused, who had given him 10s for a 2s fare. His suspicions were one of the first real leads police received.

Terry began his life of crime as a young child, when he stole sweets from other children and beat them up when they protested. Eventually, in an unusual step, Terry was moved to another school at the age of nine. At this new school he was never caned for disobedience. When he left school, Terry took up weightlifting. He was nicknamed "Muscles", and a band of admiring teenagers grew around him. However, he was the despair of his hard-working parents. Minor thieving landed him in Borstal, but he came out "talking big" in pubs, where he mainly stuck to soft drinks. He was sent back to Borstal for attacking a wage cashier, but came out even more boastful than before. He had his arms tattooed, and was moody and mean at times. He camped out often, taking a gun with him and killing rabbits, ducks and birds. One young girl was pregnant with his baby – her parents arranged a wedding – but he quickly left London and laughed off the moonlit flit. Eventually Terry arrived in Eastbourne, but moved soon afterwards to Worthing. He started taking drugs and his criminal activities began to take more shape.

Terry appealed against his death sentence, but lost on 8th May 1961. He was to be executed on 25th May that same year at Wandsworth jail in London. Five days before, it was revealed that Lloyds Bank was to pay out the £10,000 reward, but the bank would not reveal to whom. They usually gave names, but in this case one of the people who was being rewarded was worried about their identity becoming known, and the bank had agreed to respect their wishes. Meanwhile, Geoffrey Halstead, who drove Terry and Salter from Portsmouth to London, claimed that he was entitled to his share of the reward and would be seeking advice from his solicitor. This news came on the same day and shared the same newspaper space as the smaller story that Terry was due to hang. It was reported that the Home Secretary, Mr R A Butler, could find no grounds to recommend a reprieve.

The courts in November 1960 were particularly busy with regard to bank raids. On 29th November, the courage of 51-year-old bank manager John Edwards was praised twice in court when it was revealed that he had "behaved with great gallantry when faced by two armed robbers". One of the alleged gunmen told police: "I would like to say the bank manager was a very courageous man." In court in Birmingham were Derek Howell, 28, and Malcolm Jones, 32, who were accused of attempting to murder Edwards, the manager of the Birmingham Municipal Bank, and of armed robbery at the Sudbury branch of Barclays Bank, where £610 was stolen. Edwards was hit on the back of the head by the raiders as soon as he tackled them. The two masked men fled the bank empty handed, and Edwards was virtually uninjured despite two shots being fired. One of the men pointed a gun at Edwards' chest and fired, but the bullet missed, and the bank manager continued to fight. He refused to give the raiders any money, and another shot was fired.

In a brave move, Edwards lashed out with a wooden ruler. He later required two stitches in his head and had a wound on his wrist treated. He had been extremely lucky.

John Edwards had been about to close the bank for the day when two masked men walked in. One jumped on the counter with a gun in one hand and a cosh in the other, and ordered the clerk to lie face down on the floor. Then the fight with Mr Edwards took place. In court, the barrister acting for the accused told the judge that they didn't just want to apologize to the bank manager, they wanted to salute him. The two American bandits had arrived in Britain aboard the *Queen Mary*, planning to attack British banks Chicago-style. While Mr Edwards was grappling with the men, his bank clerk, Dorothy Lamin, locked herself in an office and telephoned the police. The men pleaded guilty to two bank raids and for the attempted murder of John Edwards. The judge sentenced them to 15 years in prison.

In December 1960, accountant John Bolwell broke out of a bank one weekend. To prove he wasn't having a laugh, when he went to tell police about it he took five towels and a green overall stamped with the bank's name. He had got into the bank by accident on the Saturday morning while it was still closed. He had been trying to find some friends in a block of flats near Westminster Bridge in Barnes, but got lost in a maze of corridors. Eventually he opened a door marked "Staff", and found himself in the bank's cloakroom. In a door leading into the main business chamber was a bunch of keys marked Westminster Bank. He got even more lost, and eventually climbed out of a window at the back of the bank. Having found his way in by accident – police believed him – all agreed that if John Bolwell could walk into the bank so easily it would be child's play for thieves to get in.

Meanwhile, James Torkington from Manchester received £1,000 for foiling a bank raid in the Arkwick area in September 1960.

1961 - The Jazz Pianist, the Bogus Policemen and the Missing £75,000

A gelignite gang stole £75,000 from what bank officials believed was the biggest-ever raid on a provincial bank. At Barclays Bank on Chesterton Road, Cambridge, staff arrived on 22nd March 1961 to find a hole big enough for a man to crawl through that had been blown in the 18in thick strongroom wall. Police pieced together how the gang had struck. It was believed that they had climbed in through a roof fanlight, then walked along a corridor to the boiler room. Gelignite was used to blow a hole in the brick wall separating the boiler room from the strongroom, the sound of the explosion being muffled by covering the gelignite with furniture, carpets and cushions. Raiders then squeezed through the hole (2ft by 18in wide), and forced open steel money cabinets with a jemmy before getting away with the banknotes. About £50,000 of the haul was wages for staff at Pye Radio and TV, which was based in the city. Police thought that the raiders had a tip-off about the payroll – and might also have had a sketch map of the bank. DI George Breed said: "The raid looks like the work of a London gang. It was a very professional job." The Pye employees received their wages from other banks that Friday.

The following month, Victor Woolgar heard an alarm bell sound and ran straight into the middle of a bank raid. The 35-year-old was working in his office in Park Royal Road in Harlesden, when he heard the alarm from the bank across the road. Initially he thought it was a test, but then from his office window he saw a man walking past the bank with a mask over his face. "I grabbed a spike from my desk and ran out into the road just as a second masked man came down the bank steps carrying a hold-all," he said. "I made a grab for him as he reached a car. But he immediately produced a revolver, pointed it at me and jumped into the car. As the car raced off, the bandit leaned out of the window pointing the gun in my direction. All I could do was throw the desk spike at the car. It hit it."

The two armed men escaped from the bank with £1,200 in £5 notes. Their getaway car had been stolen earlier, police later established. The men had entered the bank just as it was closing and pointed revolvers at two female clerks. Chief cashier Ronald Mann, 45, saw the men from his room at the back. He said: "I dived for the alarm bell as one of the girls screamed. Then one of the gunmen ran towards me. I dashed into the toilet, smashed the windows and jumped out to get help." The bandits grabbed the money from the tills, then ran out. Mr Mann had been present at a raid a year earlier, at which he had been bound and gagged, the robbers escaping with £5,000, and he thought that the two men were similar to the first raiders he had encountered.

In September 1961, June Hunt, 20, received a £50 reward from the National Bank for defying two men who raided their Bayswater branch. When she dialled police, one of the men fired at her, missing her by 2ft. A month later, a jazz pianist questioned in connection with the raid told a detective: "Not me, man. This is a joke. I don't dig this at all." DS Leonard Reid stated at Marylebone on 2nd October 1961 that when charged, the jazz musician replied: "I ain't saying anything." The accused was pianist Wilfred Trevor Woodley, 27, from Trinidad, and husband of actress Juliet Duncombe, whose 16-year-old brother Peter was heir to the Earl of Feversham. Woodley, who lived in Portman Square, London, was charged with the armed raid in Bayswater and with stealing £2,385. Sgt Reid told the court that two black men had entered the bank. "While one stood on the counter and threatened the staff, the other jumped over the counter and grabbed the money," he said. June Hunt, who moved to call police and was shot at, identified Woodley as the man who fired the gun. The sergeant added that he was later picked out at all three of the identification parades that were held, twice by bank employees and once by a witness who was outside the bank. Woodley was remanded and refused bail, despite being prepared to surrender his passport. Mrs Woodley, who was in court, carried the couple's baby boy in a cot to a waiting taxi, accompanied by boxer Yolande Pompey.

On 7th December 1961, Woodley was jailed and sent to Wandsworth prison for eight years for his part in the armed bank robbery. He was found guilty by an Old Bailey jury of firing the gun in the bank and taking and driving away a car, in which he escaped with an accomplice. In court was his wife Juliet, an heiress who had given Woodley a rich life. His future now looked much more frugal. She gasped when Judge Rogers told Woodley: "You have been convicted of an extremely grave matter and it is only possible for me to pass a long sentence." The court was told by Woodley that he didn't need to raid a bank because he was authorized to draw up to £30 a day from his wife's account. But Reid told the court that Woodley had been convicted in 1958 of living on immoral earnings, and was later convicted for unlawful possession of a teargas pistol. Woodley's wife was led from court sobbing.

In October 1961, the three sons of bank manager William Simpson were the most popular at their school. Everyone wanted to hear their adventure of how they watched their father get into a bogus police car and drive away, with three bank raiders posing as policemen. The boys, Robert, 18, Douglas, 15, and Graham, 14, were excited when a man phoned their home in Cunningham Park, Harrow, and said: "This is the police. The bank has been raided. A car will pick you up." When the car, a black Wolseley, arrived, the brothers went out to have a look at it – and they took the number. After the car drove off with their father, they told their mother and she phoned the police. "There's been no bank raid and we did not send a car for your husband," they said. Meanwhile, William Simpson, the 59-year-old manager of the West Smithfield (City of London) branch of the Royal Bank of Scotland, was getting suspicious. When he first got into the car, the men told him they were police officers, and they even had police messages coming over the radio, but when they got to Ludgate Circus, just before they reached the bank, the car stopped and one man got into the back and grabbed his keys, before getting out of the car and disappearing. Simpson was held on the floor of the car while it accelerated away, and after about an hour, he was thrown out in Epping Forest. The man who had Simpson's keys let himself into the bank and opened the safe's outer door. Here he found £50,000, but the raider could not get any further into the vault. In order to open the safe completely, he needed another key which was held by another member of staff. Detectives were told by an underworld tip-off that it was planned to place the loot in the carcass of a dead lamb, or bull, in Smithfield Market. The carcass would then have been met when it arrived at its destination. Simpson said, following his ordeal, that the men were fairly gentle but firm.

On 11th December 1961, the big banks paid out £16,500 in rewards in what was the first year of their "beat the gangs" campaign. Four people shared £10,000 for helping the police after the bank raid in 1960 in Worthing (as described earlier). A further £6,500 was given to 12 other people who spotted break-in attempts and told the police. Their rewards ranged from £1,000 to £50. Dorothy Davis, from Kidderminster, received £50 for telephoning the police when she saw a man on the roof of a Kidderminster bank. The police arrived as he was climbing through the window.

1962 – Bank Raid Foiled By "Mrs Mop"

A woman cleaner saved a bank thousands of pounds on 5th June 1962 by arriving at work early. It happened at the Hainault branch of Lloyds Bank in Manford Way, Chigwell, Essex. "Mrs Mop", as the newspapers dubbed her, let herself in through the front door of the bank just as a gelignite gang slipped out of the back door, leaving their equipment behind. The cleaner ran screaming from the bank to raise the alarm, and when police investigated they found gelignite already packed into the locks of the safe, carefully wrapped with old sacks to muffle the noise of the explosion. A police guard was left at the bank throughout the night, and Scotland Yard fingerprint experts were called in to help with the search for the raiders.

It wasn't quite so straightforward for a young woman in August that same year. A bandit held a broken bottle at the throat of a 24-year-old expectant mother while his companion grabbed £3,000 in a bank raid. Lorna Wright walked into the Westminster Bank at Great Barr, Birmingham to cash a cheque. She was followed in by two men. One gripped Lorna by the neck and held the bottle to her throat, saying to 19-year-old cashier Patricia Brookes: "If you ring the alarm, she'll get this in the throat ... and you'll get it next." The other raider leapt over the counter and shovelled banknotes into a bag, and then the two men ran out and escaped in a car. Lorna Wright, who was expecting her first baby, said: "I did not scream or shout. I just stood still and I could feel myself trembling. It was terrifying."

Another civilian who showed tremendous courage was bank clerk Peter Crimmins, 28, who battled with a gunman who had already shot down a guard. He was awarded an MBE for his actions. Crimmins disarmed the man and then clubbed him with the raider's sawn-off shotgun. The citation, published in the *London Gazette* on 25th September 1962, told the story of how ex-Gordonstoun schoolboy Archie Trew walked into the branch of the Westminster Bank at Banwell, Somerset. Crimmins was there with bank guard Bob Wallis, 68. Trew demanded money before shooting Mr Wallis. Crimmins, of Burnham-on-Sea, tackled Trew, and as he fought for the gun the second barrel went off, but the shot hit the wall. When Crimmins finally got the gun, he hit Trew over the head with it repeatedly until the gunman weakened. Crimmins then forced Trew into the street, and grappled with him in the gutter until help arrived. Bob Wallis died five hours later, and Trew was found guilty at Hampshire Assizes of manslaughter. He was jailed for 10 years.

A 22-year-old police motorcyclist who ran down another bank raider was awarded the BEM. PC Walter Bonner of Liverpool City Police saw a man with a revolver being chased after a bank raid. He drove at the man and knocked him down, then jumped on him and held him until other police arrived. The raider, Ronald Naif, 20, was jailed for 14 years for armed robbery.

More bravery was shown in December when a 40-year-old bank clerk crawled on his hands and knees to raise the alarm in a £10,000 bank raid. Two masked and armed men burst into the Westminster Bank in Isleworth at 2.20pm, herded customers into a corner and began to threaten staff. Then they threatened the counter clerk, Joyce Malbey, 19, and demanded money. Cashier Donald Killick, 18, leapt over the counter to grapple with the gunmen, but one bandit pointed the gun at him and said: "Get back or I'll blow your brains out." The bandits were distracted by Joyce, who was rude to them, and as she spoke, her colleague, Mr A H Lawrence, crawled to the door. Once he had disappeared from view, he opened the back door and ran to phone the police. The bandits snatched the money from behind the grille and disappeared into the fog. Bank manager Arthur Gaster said: "The staff did all they possibly could to prevent them getting away with the money. I am very proud of them."

1963 – A Handsome Rogue and the Pick-Handle Gang

Ludwik Urbas, a rogue Romeo in a red sports car, captivated 17-year-old typist Marilyn Day with his grand manner and good looks. He took her for a five-month jaunt around the country, but the teenager had no idea that the money he spent so freely came from a life of crime. The jaunt brought them both to the Old Bailey dock on 18th March 1963, and there the lovers parted company.

Belgian-born Urbas, 33, was sent to jail for eight years for bank robbery, car theft and forging cheques. Marilyn was set free – cleared of a charge of helping Urbas in the bank robbery. She did not know that when she met Urbas in a coffee bar in August 1962 that he was already wanted by British and Continental police. Nor did she know that he had a number of girlfriends across Europe, or that, as they drove around the West Country together, he was forging cheques to pay their way. Marilyn Day was also unaware that when Urbas wanted to satisfy his craving for fast sports cars he simply walked into a showroom and drove one away while the staff weren't looking. Marilyn became involved in the bank robbery when Urbas drove her to Kingsbury, Middlesex, and left her in a car parked in a side street. He went by underground train to the next station, stole another car and drove it back to Kingsbury. Then, armed with a starting pistol, he held up a Midland Bank cashier and scooped £563 from the counter. He made his getaway in the car in which Marilyn had waited. The couple were later arrested at Lydney, Gloucestershire. Prosecuting counsel at the Old Bailey said there was nothing to show that Marilyn Day did anything to help the bank robbery. No evidence was offered against her, and she was formally acquitted. She went home with her parents to Dunstable, Bedfordshire.

In September 1963, the pick-handle gang made their third raid on a London bank in a week. Five men attacked the manager and a cashier at Lloyds Bank in Croxted Road, Dulwich, and escaped in a stolen car with several hundred pounds. The bank officials were not badly hurt. A fortnight later, on 26th September 1963, the gang were back again. The gang of six waited until Barclays Bank in Brockley Road, Brockley, emptied just before closing time. Then five of them, carrying pick handles, ran in, and the remaining man stayed in the car. Three of the bandits threatened the staff, while two of them vaulted the counter and snatched £1,000 from the till. One of the raiders set off a "dust screen" by releasing a fire extinguisher at the staff. Moments later, the gang dashed back to the car and made off towards Catford. A young man on a motorbike chased the gang, but gave up when the car stopped and two men got out and ran towards him. No one was injured, though a female cashier fainted during the raid.

Six-year-old Paul Norrington received £25 reward money when he foiled a bank raid. He chose to spend his money on a toy traction engine. "I wanted a steam engine more than anything else in the world," he said on 19th November 1963. Paul lived with his family two doors away from a branch of National Provincial Bank in Upper High Street, Epsom. He was woken one night when the bank's burglar alarm went off. He ran to his parents' bedroom, woke his father and told him to phone the police. Within minutes, squad cars were at the bank and the gang, all set to blow open the safe, was surrounded. All the raiders were arrested. The bank manager, who heard that it was Paul that stopped the raid, asked to see the little boy's father and gave him the £25. In the end Paul spent some of the money on the engine, but with the remainder chose to open a savings account – at the National Provincial Bank.

1964 – Shot in Raid, but Bank Hero Fought Back, and Time for Tea

Shorthand typist Anne Newman walked straight into a bank raid on 27th February 1964. A masked robber grabbed her by the waist and said: "It's all right, dear. Don't worry." Then 17-year-old Anne was forced at gunpoint to stand with her hands above her head – alongside the bank manager and a cashier – as the six-man gang scooped £52,000 from a strongroom. The raid, carried out in 10 minutes, was at Barclays Bank in New Kent Road, Southwark. Messenger Frank Fox, 36, was coshed by the raiders, who had concealed themselves in the basement before the bank opened. The gang were known to police as the "Inside Mob". Anne Newman said: "I went down to the vaults with a message for the manager, when suddenly a lot of men rushed up behind me. One of them put his arm around my waist." He told her not to worry. She continued: "I was shaking with fright – it was like a nightmare. The gang leader told us to put our hands up as two of the men bundled notes into three sacks. Then they suddenly stopped and simply hopped it." The gang, wearing nylon stocking masks and carrying pick handles, were thought to have got into the bank early the day before through an adjourning office block. There was no sign of a break-in. They had crept into a disused room near the iron-grilled strongroom and waited until manager Frederick Woodward and cashier

Ronald Shrubsole went down to open the vaults.

On 15th May 1964, however, it was revealed that bank messenger Frank Fox had joined in the plot to rob his bank. To avoid suspicion, he arranged to be hit on the head; later, he was to share in the loot. Fox, though, lost out all round. He was hit much harder than he expected as the other plotters made their getaway, and his head wound needed six stitches. He never collected a penny of the haul – and was then jailed at the Old Bailey for his part in the raid for four years. Fox, from Bermondsey, had provided the gang with a key which enabled the robbers to reach the strongroom without any difficulty. It might never have been suspected that he was part of the gang if he hadn't dropped some keys – not the bank's – in the street, and a passer-by hadn't taken them to the police. While being questioned after the robbery, Fox lied to the police about the keys he had lost. They became suspicious, and then he confessed about providing a key for the raiders. A jury at the Old Bailey failed to reach a verdict in the case in which three men were charged with conspiring to rob the bank. A new trial was planned.

Unlike Fox, another bank employee was badly injured and fought back in a raid in May. The bullet, fired by a "woman in red", hit bank clerk Brennan Cran, 25, in the chest. But he refused to give in, a court was told, and desperately, courageously, fought back – and wrenched the gun from the woman at the bank in Darlington, County Durham. It was then that he realized the raider was a man in women's clothes. Brennan then tried to shoot the raider in the leg to foil a getaway, but the gun wouldn't fire. Despite feeling faint, because of his loss of blood having been shot, he grappled with the man instead. A bank guard dashed to help and soon the raider was overpowered. In court, accused of attempting to murder Brennan and rob him, was garage owner Dennis Turnbull, 35, of Girsby, Yorkshire. Edward Freeman, for the prosecution, said that Turnbull went to Barclays Bank in North Road, Darlington, wearing a woman's dark brown wig, a complete outfit of women's clothes, including underclothes, and a red mac. He planned to return to his garage after the robbery and change his clothes. Turnbull entered the bank with a gun and announced: "This is a hold-up." Brennan told the court that on the "woman's" orders he put money into a carrier bag. He was asked how much money there was, so proceeded to count it slowly. The frustrated gunman then forced Brennan into the bank's safe room at gunpoint, and a bank guard sounded the alarm. Then, said Brennan, "the person fired from about a yard away". The hearing was adjourned.

It was announced in October 1964 that Brennan Cran had been awarded the George Medal for his bravery. "Although seriously wounded, Cran grappled with the man, grabbed the gun and hit him on the forehead with it. Cran was by now in a state of collapse, but retained his hold until the police arrived and arrested the gunman," said newspaper reports. Cran had several emergency operations to save his life. He did, however, return to the same branch when he was well enough. Bank guard James Greenwood, 67, who had sounded the alarm, was awarded the Queen's Commendation for brave conduct, as did removal man Fred Scott, who as a passer-by had helped the two men in the ensuing struggle.

In June, raiders took the unusual step of making themselves a cup of tea. They blasted their way into a bank strongroom and helped themselves to £24,000, before boiling the water for a pot of tea on a gas ring. Before leaving the bank, they washed up the staff cups they had used. A senior detective said: "This was not a sign of tidiness – they wanted to remove their fingerprints." The raiders were believed to have spent most of a Sunday inside the bank – the National Provincial – in Kidderminster, Worcestershire; the robbery wasn't discovered until the staff arrived to open up on Monday 22nd June. The thieves first forced their way into the derelict Lion Hotel next door, as the first floor stretched over the bank. The men hacked a hole in the floor and climbed down a ladder through the bank's ceiling into a toilet. Their first attempt to blow the door of the basement strongroom failed, but a second gelignite charge shattered part of the strongroom's wall. Squeezing through a hole, they blew open two safes to get to the money. To open the quadruple-locked main safe, they let off detonators in two of the keyholes. In making their getaway, they left behind a ladder and two crowbars. Worcestershire's CID chief, DS Harry Parley, said: "It is almost certain the thieves took their gear to the bank in a vehicle. Anyone who saw the vehicle standing in the street, normally deserted on a Sunday, should contact me immediately." The police chief also asked lodging-house keepers in the area to report any casual weekend guests. That same weekend, thieves stole at least £70,000 worth of jewels in Glasgow from a shop by blowing open three of the firm's four safes. They also used an oxyacetylene cutter, taking their equipment along in a golfing bag.

In August 1978 safe-breaker Donald Mather walked into a Nottingham police station, asked to see a detective for whom he had a "high regard", and confessed his part in the Kidderminster bank robbery, 14 years after the raid. The guilty secret had preyed on his mind more and more as time went by. By the time of his confession, Worcester Crown Court was told on 19th January 1979, Mather couldn't remember in which year the robbery had taken place – and the bank itself had long since been demolished, the site being redeveloped. Mather admitted to stealing nearly £25,000. Prosecutor John West said: "The police had a very good idea who had done it. But there was no hard evidence and no arrests were ever made." Simon Brand, defending, said: "This is a remarkable case – one in a lifetime. Mather really wants a fresh start and to clean the slate completely." Mather, who had been jailed for 10 years in 1966 for theft and using explosives, and by this time was living with his sister in Shrewsbury, was remanded on bail for reports. On 27th February 1979, he walked free, although he had hoped he would be sent to jail. He told police: "Life's a right rat race. I'd be better off inside." His hopes of a stretch behind bars were dashed by Judge John Lee. He gave the grey-haired Mather a two-year suspended sentence: "You are at an age when people with your sort of record see middle age ahead of them and are able to settle down." Mather should have got 10 to 12 years for his part in the robbery, the judge said, but he had stayed away from crime for seven years before his confession. "Although this may seem an odd way of doing justice, I think justice has been done," added Judge Lee.

1965 – New Hunt for the Great Train Robbers

In February 1965, police stepped up their hunt for the members of the Great Train Robbery gang who were still at large. The move followed a "brilliant" bank raid, in which it was estimated that cash and jewels amounting to between £100,000 and £1m were stolen. It took place at a Lloyds branch in Knightsbridge, where 50 trunks, cases and packets deposited in the strongroom were rifled. The raiders got into the room by using a new device known as a thermic lance, a fiercely burning torch which could cut through almost any known metal at a terrific speed. One customer put his personal loss at £50,000 in cash and jewels. But it was thought that the full value of the raid might never be known, as it was believed that some of the deposit owners had died. A senior police officer said: "We immediately thought that this raid could be connected with the Great Train Robbery. The bank raid was a brilliant operation. We have an idea who might be the brains behind it." One theory was that the strongroom deposits included Great Train Robbery money. This tied in with a theory that part of the massive haul was deposited in banks in innocent-looking cases. The gang were believed to have been tipped off that their hideaway was about to be uncovered.

In a bizarre case, it was discovered that cartridges fired into the ceiling during a bank raid had been filled with rice. A court was told of the strange finding at the end of February 1965. It was believed that the bank raiders may have thought that firing rice wouldn't hurt anybody. However, prosecutor Geoffrey Leach in Marylebone said that tests showed the grains of rice could kill at short range. This was confirmed by John McCafferty, an experimental officer from Scotland Yard. The rice cartridges were fired from a shotgun during one of four raids carried out by a gang on London banks in 19 days. They used stolen cars, and two of the four men who entered each bank leapt onto the counter to raid the till, it was alleged. Frederick Sanson, 31, from East Dulwich was accused of taking part in bank raids in Islington, Southwark, Hornsey and Wood Green; the total haul was £7,000. In May 1965, Frederick Sanson's barrister failed to turn up in court and was severely reprimanded by Judge Carl Aarvold, who told Harold Lester that he had "failed in his duties". The judge said: "While there was perhaps little that you could say or do to help your client, he was at least entitled to the comfort of your presence and of your support at the time of his conviction and sentence." He continued: "He failed to have either and that must be a cause of deep regret and shame to you." Lester apologized, and said he had been under the impression that his junior, Edward St George, would be in court when the jury returned their verdict. The judge accepted the apology. Sanson was jailed for 12 years, having appeared in the dock alongside Mark Owens, 31, who was with him on three of the raids. Owens was jailed for 10 years.

On 27th December 1966, more than 18 months after Sanson was sent to prison, Raymond Hanney, 26, one of five men known as the "Boxing Day escapers", who had escaped from Dartmoor prison, was recaptured after the car he was driving crashed through a police roadblock. This was formed by a police car and another vehicle that were blocking the A38 Exeter to Plymouth road between Benedict's Bridge and Chudleigh Knighton, Devon. Hanney hit the police car at speed in a Mini Traveller estate car taken from Dartmeet, in the middle of Dartmoor – and raced off along the road. The police car was too badly damaged to give chase, but a radio warning alerted another roadblock 5 miles away. As Hanney, of Peckham, reached this, he stopped. Police arrested him without a struggle. Hanney was still wearing his jail clothes, and a policeman said: "He was soaked to the skin." The recapture came as a warning was being flashed to police that another of the Boxing Day escapers, Mark Owens, a former boxing champion, should not be tackled single-handed. Throughout the previous day, 300 prison officers, policemen with dogs and Royal Marine Commandos had searched Dartmoor for the escapers, supported by two Army Air Corps spotter helicopters. Hanney and Owens had escaped with John Johnson, 30, John Thompson, 28, and James Morey, 23. The men – known to friends as the London Mob – escaped from the jail's gym after overpowering a prison officer and a physical training instructor, and their escape was regarded as the worst in a year. When a farmer found beer bottles and the remains of chocolates as well as a portable radio at Chardstock, close to Crediton, north-west of Exeter, the search for the remaining missing men changed direction.

In September 1965, publican's wife Doris Roe glanced out of

her kitchen window and saw a team of robbers walking into the National Provincial Bank across the road. She immediately phoned police, while her husband, Fred, 44, licensee of The George, Woodford Green, ran over and looked through a window, to see the gang holding up the bank with a sawn-off shotgun. Roe intended to follow the gang, but by the time he had got his car out they had vanished, escaping with £10,000 in notes in a black bag from the safe – which had been unlocked as staff prepared for the day's business. As they fled in a blue Ford Zephyr, they knocked down a cyclist and later crashed into a van. The gang then ran to a petrol station, where they stole an estate car as the driver got out to fill it up.

The following month, with brakes squealing, a police car cut in front of a taxi moving down a side street, whille another one pulled up behind. The police were hot on the trail of a gang of masked raiders who had got away with £4,000 from a London bank a few minutes earlier. They hauled out the taxi driver, five protesting young men and a woman and frisked them. Then there was an embarrassed silence. The police hadn't managed to catch the thieves but a pop group. It was 18-year-old Beryl Marsden and the Crew, a new London-based group on their way to an appointment with a *Mirror* photographer. Howie Casey, 21-year-old leader of the Crew, said they were running late for the photoshoot, so they asked the taxi driver to take a short cut to the *Mirror* building in Holborn. Suddenly, however, the group was surrounded by police. The police apologized.

Meanwhile, the raiders, their faces hidden by stocking masks, escaped in a stolen green Jaguar. They used ammonia-filled water pistols and an iron bar in their snatch at Lloyds Bank, Cricklewood Broadway. Two of the gang vaulted the front counter and grabbed bundles of notes from open drawers. Three bank clerks – Philip Collins, Wallis Urry and Anthony Pugsley – were injured, but were allowed home following treatment in hospital.

1966 – George Medal for Bank Hero and a Run of Bad Luck

Fred Williams only had a small job but some very big ideas. These ideas added up to a fantastic plot – to pull off the world's biggest bank robbery. Williams, an odd job man at the head office of Lloyds Bank in London, thought over the details as he pottered about his work. He dreamed of a life of luxury ... a fortune almost too vast to spend. And it could all so easily have come true. Unluckily for the 45-year-old, who had been feted as a hero after he told of foiling an eight-man gang in a bank raid, he talked over his idea with one person too many. After an underworld tip-off, detectives set up an ambush near the bank on the day the big raid was due to take place.

At 7.30am, Williams carried a sack across to the bank. Later an oxygen cylinder was found inside it, and an oxyacetylene cutting gun was found in a broom cupboard. Detectives found four keys on Williams, which unlocked two grille doors leading to the strongroom. Michael Wilkinson, defending Williams at the Old Bailey in March 1966 on a conspiracy charge, said: "He fell under the influence of men playing for high stakes." Williams learned the cost of his gamble when he was jailed for five years.

In late July, six armed men took one look at a lone policeman on a bike and changed their minds about a bank raid. The raid that never was began when a stolen Jaguar was driven onto the pavement outside the Uxbridge Road branch of Barclays Bank, Hayes. Six men with pick handles and an axe poured out and ran to the bank doors. At the same time, PC William Mossey cruised up on his bike. The startled gang took a quick look, did an about turn and ran for it. Inside the bank, business continued as usual. Mossey followed them, but he had no chance of catching the speeding car, which was found abandoned in Southall. Inside was a holdall containing masks, two axes and a shotgun. Police took the car away for fingerprint examinations.

Building worker David Coppin, 26, foiled a bank raid by four youths – one of whom was armed with a shotgun – and was awarded the George Medal. First he moved their car to hinder their getaway from the bank in Ealing, then showed extreme bravery by grabbing the armed raider and handing him over to police. In May 1966, Coppin, from Purley, Surrey, was awarded £1,000 reward for his actions by the Committee of London Clearing Banks.

By November 1966, waiter Pepino Pollie, 24, had saved up for two years to buy his dream car – a sky blue Alfa-Romeo. Finally, he had the £850 he needed, but his dream soon turned to a nightmare. Pepino took a holiday from his restaurant job in Carlisle, and flew to Naples to buy the car. He drove it back to Britain, but found that there was excess customs duty to pay of £400, so he took a train the 300 miles to Carlisle and borrowed the cash from his boss. Meanwhile the customs demand had gone up another £50, because of a mistake. He had no choice but to drive the car back to Naples and try to sell it – but by then the car's value had dropped £250. Pepino rang a motoring organization, which promised to help him get the car into Britain. He set off north again, but on the way his insurance ran out. He stepped into a phone box to arrange for the railway to transport the car for him, and when he returned to his car it had vanished, along with his passport. The police told him: "You cannot leave Italy till the passport turns up." For three weeks he wandered around Milan. Eventually, the police found his car: it had been used in a bank raid.

1967 – Workmen Crack a Strongroom to Let Their Mate Out

A gang of men drilled hastily through the roof of a bank's strongroom on 5th January 1967. They tied ropes to the door and heaved and tugged, until at last it gave way. Out of the strongroom, pale and shocked, staggered one of their own workmates. The bank raid that never was had begun with a prank: a workman had shut the door on plaster's mate John Charlton. The 1½ ton steel door had not been hung properly, and when it slammed shut it stayed shut. The workmen, who were building a new branch of the Midland Bank in Longfleet, Dorset, decided that there was only one option: to break in. It took them an hour to drill through the roof so that Charlton could breathe, then another three hours to get the door open.

On 14th July 1967, police revealed the face of a killer. It was the latest picture of the man who, detectives thought, had murdered a "have a go" hero, Tony Fletcher, during a bank raid. The drawing was thought to be more like the wanted man than an earlier picture released, being prepared from descriptions by people who had witnessed an armed robbery in Covent Garden the day before a Chelsea bank raid two weeks earlier. Police were satisfied that the same man was involved in both crimes. Tony Fletcher, 33, was shot dead when he tried to catch the Chelsea gunman.

1968 – The Case of the Dead Bank Manager Shot by Police

David Payne, 19, wanted to buy himself out of the Army to return home to help his mother, so he decided to stage a bank raid in London to get the necessary £250. He walked into the National Bank in Baker Street, and pulled out an imitation Luger pistol. But, the manager, Mr T T Cowling, knocked the weapon from Payne's hand and put a half nelson grip on him. Then the police were called. Payne, a lance-corporal in the Royal Army Ordnance Corps, had decided to stage his "hold-up" when he was stationed in Germany, the Old Bailey heard. His defence counsel said that Payne had been worried about his mother because she was seeking a divorce. Payne pleaded guilty to possessing an imitation firearm. A plea of not guilty to attempting an armed robbery was accepted, and he was given a conditional discharge.

However, things were much more serious in November 1968 in New Jersey, USA. Police shot a bank manager dead by mistake as they waited in ambush for a gang of raiders. The manager, 27-year-old Douglas Tyler, had been taken prisoner by the gang after they entered his bank in Cinnaminson, New Jersey. They handcuffed him and pushed him into a back room, but unknown to the three raiders, who were disguised in dark glasses and false moustaches, one of the staff triggered a silent alarm and police surrounded the bank. When Tyler realized the police were outside, he made a break for it and dashed, still handcuffed, through the door. He was cut down with a shotgun blast by one of the policemen. A spokesman said afterwards: "He just burst out of the door. One of our men ordered him to stop, but he didn't." The three raiders were later captured and charged with armed robbery.

Back in Britain, later that month, four bandits – one posing as an Electricity Board inspector – got away with £80,000 in a bank raid at Barclays Bank at the Royal Albert Dock. They escaped with the money stuffed in brown paper bags. The raid began at 2.15pm when a man in a dark blue uniform walked in and introduced himself as an inspector. After a 10-minute talk with the assistant manager, the bogus inspector was allowed behind the counter. At that moment, three masked men brandishing guns burst in. The imposter then helped the other raiders to tie up the three bank employees, before they took the money from the strongroom and escaped in a car. It took the bank employees 10 minutes to free themselves and raise the alarm.

On 1st December 1968, the police stepped up a nationwide hunt for three armed men, all thought to be in their 20s, and a blonde woman, described as being around 18 years old, who smashed through a roadblock in a 100mph chase. The three men had escaped from custody while waiting to appear in court on charges of armed robbery. They stole five cars – one at gunpoint – as police pursued them across the West Country. The men were wanted for questioning about a £20,000 bank raid in Birmingham.

The drama began after an underworld tip to police that the gang had left Birmingham in a stolen Jaguar. Detectives set an ambush at Swindon, and a police car spotted the Jaguar on a country road. The fast and furious chase began. A sawn-off shotgun was thrust through a window of the stolen car and pointed at the following police. But when the cars hit a straight stretch of road, the Jag accelerated to more than 100mph and got away. A warning went out to Bristol police that the car was heading their way, and it was later found crashed at Lansdown Place, in the Clifton area of the city. A Mini which had been parked nearby was missing. The hunt started in earnest.

The gang stopped the Mini in the Sea Mills area of Bristol, and held up the owner of a Ford Anglia with their shotgun. They took his car and drove off, but were spotted at Almondsbury, Gloucestershire. There they outpaced police in another high-speed chase, and when the Anglia ran out of petrol they stole a Morris 1100, evading police by smashing through a roadblock. A few minutes later, the Morris was found near Gromhall, 10 miles from Bristol. The gang then stole another car a mile away.

Armed detectives waited on 2nd December to make their final swoop on the gang as the massive hunt turned its focus to London. The bronze Ford Zodiac – which the gang stole on their way back through Gloucestershire – was spotted empty in Paddington, and squads of detectives with search warrants – some carrying guns – ringed the area, waiting to move in. The police had the addresses of associates of the three men, who were named by Scotland Yard as Roger Dennhardt, 20, Terence Tharme, 20, and Christopher Hague, 19. All three hailed from West London. The woman was not named. Police thought that the gang had split into pairs and gone into hiding at the homes of friends. They were believed to have plenty of ammunition for the two shotguns they possessed, and Scotland Yard warned anyone spotting the men that "under no circumstances are they to try to detain them". The first sign of the gang had been in the early hours, when a woman phoned the AA to say that a bronze Zodiac had broken down in Watford High Street. The police were informed, but the car had gone by the time they arrived. It was believed that the men were evading capture by listening in to police radio messages. Meanwhile, it was revealed that the gang were also responsible for a raid in West Hanwell in August.

The parents of two of the youths appealed to them to give themselves up on 3rd December, when the mother of Terence Tharme and the father of Roger Dennhardt appeared on ITV's *News at Ten*. The two parents had been "anxious" to appear. The hunt then moved to Yorkshire and Cheshire.

On 4th December, Sandra Shelton, the girlfriend of Hague, was named by Scotland Yard, and two photographs of her were issued in the hope that they might help to trap the men. Sandra, who had bleached blonde hair, was known to wear dark wigs, which changed her appearance completely. The Yard said that she was known to be with the wanted men, and that they were aware that Tharme and Hague had stayed overnight in a Leeds hotel. Their stay was kept secret for 24 hours in the hope that they were still in the city, but it seemed they had moved on. Scotland Yard also named Francis Farren, 20, whom they believed had joined the four fugitives. Farren had called at a house in Rochdale, Lancashire, just days earlier. By 6th December, however, the hunt had moved to Halifax, Yorkshire, where two of the men and Sandra had been seen drinking in a pub. Dennhardt and Farren were not with them. Police appealed to the gang to give themselves up: "We are anxious to avoid violence and we strongly urge them to get in touch with the police at a police station or with New Scotland Yard, so that their safe conduct may be assured. If they wish to do so, they can telephone Detective Chief Superintendent Frank Davies." It was the biggest hint yet that as a last resort the police were prepared to use whatever force was necessary to recapture the gang members.

Heather Wilks – whose photograph was mistakenly released to the press and described as Sandra wearing a dark wig – had had a brief friendship with some of the gang members. She had met Farren, who called himself Mike Bart, in the street, along with Tharme, who called himself Terry Elliot. Heather said that the youths, in a Jag, "chatted up" the girls in Bristol. She described them as "nice, ordinary blokes", and said that she and her girlfriends saw them three or four times a week. Heather had come forward after seeing her own picture on the television, which had been taken by Hague when she was washing dishes in the lads' flat. Police then released a picture of Dennhardt kissing Christine Mason, an 18-year-old typist, and sat at her home waiting for her young lover to call – as he had done once already during his time on the run. Christine, from Cranford, was reported to have agreed to marry Dennhardt if he gave himself up, and he had promised to ring her again with his decision. As the eight-day hunt continued, on 8th December, police were searching for a man they believed had vital information about the gang. He had written a letter, posted in Birmingham, which reached the *Daily Mirror*. This suggested that the gang's tempers were becoming frayed, and that at least one of them might be about to give himself up: it was thought that the four youths had had a row over money, and about Sandra. The letter said: "He [the gang member] is breezed up and looks like squealing any time now." It was signed with the name of a man known to police. Meanwhile, Sandra's father, Harry Shelton, was convinced that his daughter was being held captive. On 9th December, the gang's car was found abandoned at a tube station in London, and the gang were thought to be lying low close to Earl's Court. It was reported that they had come back to the capital after stealing a green Ford Zephyr from Derby. Finally, on 16th December, Tharme was arrested in Hammersmith. He was later charged with causing grievous bodily harm to a prison officer at Ashford remand centre (from where he had escaped with the other three men), and was due in court on the 17th of the month. The other three youths already stood charged with the same crime. Dennhardt, Hague and Tharme, having broken out of Ashford remand centre in 1968, were sentenced in April 1969 with up to five years each.

In September 1981, it was reported that Roger Dennhardt

had had it made by 1976. Each of his four bank accounts stood comfortably in four or five figures. He zipped around London in fast cars and was popular with women. At the age of 28, he had reached the pinnacle of his craft – armed robbery. Dennhardt was holding up banks, security firms and shops two or three times a week when his career of crime came to a sudden stop: he found a gun muzzle pressed to his own head, having walked into a police trap. In jail, the master criminal had time to reflect on his corrupt past. And after three years he turned informer.

Dennhardt had been one of the hardest, most ruthless, most accomplished bandits of his generation; now he was a supergrass. His information put dozens of crooks in prison, and resulted in the recovery of cash and stolen property worth hundreds of thousands of pounds. He applied himself to his new role with all the vigour and dedication he had spent on his criminal career. The task of unloading such a mass of names and numbers was aided by a near-photographic memory; that and the attention to detail which had served him so well during the years of crime.

Dennhardt had thought of himself, with some justification, as the most highly skilled robber in the land: a thorough professional. His particular strength was planning – dealing with the intricacies of vehicles, weapons, approach and escape routes, the back-up operation and the habits of victims. To his diligent mind, the "work" could not be considered over until all possibilities of retribution had faded. A professional also had to be prepared to deal with the aftermath of his deeds as painstakingly as he had dealt with the preparations. He had to be skilled at manufacturing false evidence and bribing jurors (or policemen) as he might be at persuading a terrified bank clerk to open a safe or at piloting a getaway car. Dennhardt stood high in the ranks of villainy. Before he was 20, he was acknowledged as "a face" – a criminal celebrity. At his peak he ran a black and white Camaro and a blue BMW. He might go from a meeting with respectful colleagues to his tailor; from a rendezvous in a discreet afternoon club to a gaudy disco. Pernod and lemonade was drunk sparingly. He was tall, muscular, serious-looking, and he looked after himself. He took care too of his girl, Melissa, a 15-year-old pale-skinned brunette, who had an endearing way of doing what she was told. Night after night – and often in broad daylight – Dennhardt changed his sharp suit for the sinister rig of his true calling and took up the lethal tools of his trade. On the job that brought about his downfall – a £34,000 raid on a security van in Hemel Hempstead – he carried a pump-action shotgun. One of the stolen getaway cars led police to the man they wanted, and he was arrested in February 1977. He began a 13-year jail sentence. The morning of the arrest in Islington, he and Melissa had made love after patching up a quarrel; he could still smell her on his skin as police made their arrest. Despite having taken part in a series of crimes that netted nearly £1m over more than a decade, going QE – Queen's Evidence – earned Dennhardt his freedom. He took refuge from underworld revenge with a new identity and a new appearance, and moved from his old haunts to start a life abroad – leaving behind what he hoped was a "positive contribution" to the fight against crime.

He said: "During the past three years I have wrestled with a strong desire to confess my crimes and to a great extent put right the immense damage I have inflicted ... It really is the only honourable course a man such as myself has left to take. I am totally friendless now. I have caused a major schism within my own family. This act of informing is the most positive proof I can give that I have concluded my criminal career forever." Dennhardt's statements to the police took five months to record and amazed his interrogators. He lectured for hours on the way in which his fellow villains ordered their eccentric lives, on their taste in clothes and entertainment, their children and their women. It was an eye-opener even for the police. Dennhardt had become hooked on a criminal way of life early on: he found it easy and loved the power it gave him. Crime was better than working; above all, it made him feel like a somebody. His unstable childhood contained all the classic ingredients: warring parents, fear of his father's violence, non-existent home life, inconsistent supervision and bad company. He had the same probation officer at the age of 15 that his father had had for an assault on his mother: he had watched at the age of nine as his mother's head was bashed against a wall.

Dennhardt's confession led to police solving more than 300 crimes and putting more than 40 villains behind bars. In return, he was freed from the 13-year jail sentence that was imposed on him. He changed his name to Paul Cannon, and bought a club and restaurant in Exmouth.

Almost 10 years after giving up crime, Dennhardt was once again sought by police after an unsuccessful £300,000 armed robbery on a Post Office van in Aldershot, Hampshire, in January 1986. The policeman assigned as his minder was in custody, accused of taking part in the same hold-up. Dennhardt, it was believed, had escaped to France with his girlfriend, Sharon, having vanished the day after the raid. Police also wanted to interview him in connection with a raid on a Post Office van in Mansfield, Nottinghamshire, when robbers escaped with £307,000. After the Aldershot raid, Dennhardt's Lancia had been spotted nearby. Police watching his Exmouth club ambushed his car, but he reversed and escaped. He said that he thought the police were robbers out to get him: his supergrass status had not gone down well in the underworld. He also claimed that he had been in Aldershot to try and sell his car at an auction. However, DS Graham Sayer, from Thames Valley, who had been assigned to act as Dennhardt's minder, was charged with taking part in the Post Office van raid, and was refused bail when he appeared before magistrates: he was eventually jailed for nine years, and hung his head in shame in November 1986 when he was found guilty. Sayer had become close friends with Dennhardt when assigned to mind him, and had been drawn into the raider's web of criminal activities. Sayer was expected to be held in solitary confinement for his own protection. The 14-times commended former policeman had single-handedly cracked a multi-million-pound drug ring before befriending Dennhardt, but with his marriage on the rocks and facing early retirement because of a back injury, he turned into a gangster alongside Dennhardt and became his willing accomplice. It was a painful end to a glittering career on the right side of the law.

While Dennhardt was enjoying notoriety in 1968, widow Kate Moody, 68, popped into the Midland Bank in Upper Brentwood Road, Essex, on 4th December to cash a cheque, and walked into her third bank raid at the branch in a year. The raid had targeted a crew of Security Express guards taking £15,500 in wages to workers on a local building site. Two sharply dressed men hid themselves inside the bank before the guards arrived, and as they moved out with the money, the two raiders pounced. A third bandit joined the scuffle, and a blank was fired from a shotgun. The gang escaped in a white Austin driven by a fourth man; it was later found abandoned. Kate Moody said later at her nearby home that it was excitement that at her age she could well do without. She described how she had nearly collapsed with fright, and had to be given a glass of water in a butcher's shop next door. She described the ordeal as "a dreadful experience".

A newspaper report a day later said of another raid: "As a bank raid, it only needed the Keystone Cops to complete the slapstick." The *Mirror* was referring to the raid which started ominously enough when three masked men carrying ammonia guns burst into a Midland Bank branch in High Street, Knowle, Warwickshire. Before they demanded anything, the counter clerks set off the alarm bells. The din was deafening. The raiders panicked and fled, but not smartly enough to catch up with their getaway car. As they reached the pavement outside the bank, the car was vanishing up the street: the three masked bandits were left stranded. It was, of course, no place for them to be loitering for long, so they ran away, chased by several shoppers, and dashed into the playground of an infants' school 300yds from the bank. There they grabbed three bikes, and pedalled off in a hurry. Their antics were observed by a trio of eight-year-old girls dressed as angels for their Christmas play, who ran to tell the headmaster that three men had stolen the dinner ladies' bikes. The girls then wrote out descriptions of the men. The would-be bank raiders – reduced to bicycle thieves – did not pedal very far: the bikes were later found a few hundred yards away. The non-getaway car was also found abandoned. "As bank robbers, they wouldn't make the fifth division," said Chief Inspector George Forsythe.

1969 – Bank Raid Gunmen Force a Policeman to Beg for his Life

A young policeman who thought he was going to be executed was made to kneel in a road and beg for his life on 6th March 1969. PC Douglas Hogg, 28, was ambushed by a gang of gunmen after £13,000 was stolen in two bank raids. With him in his police car was an off-duty PC, John McClung, 29, who had seen one of the raids – in Newry, County Down, Northern Ireland. The gunmen repeatedly fired at the pursuing police during a 70mph chase. After driving into a trap – and a hail of bullets – the police car was rammed by one of the gang's cars. McClung crawled away to get help as PC Hogg was dragged out of the car. After pleading for his life, PC Hogg was hit on the head with the rifle before the raiders drove off.

Three men who were arrested in an attempted bank raid claimed that the robbery was a put-up job. It was suggested to them by an "informer" who hoped to get a reward from the bank, they told a court on 14th March 1969. But a judge at the Old Bailey said that their story made no difference to their guilt. "You thought you were taking part in a genuine robbery," Judge King Hamilton told the men. "You armed yourselves with imitation firearms and metal coshes as well. Your moral guilt is exactly the same." The men had been caught in a Flying Squad ambush at the Westminster Bank in Havering, Essex. John Miah, 24, was jailed for six years and six months of a suspended sentence. John Bracken, 27, was jailed for five years and Peter Gregory, 24, for four years, to follow an 18-month sentence already passed on him for factory breaking. The men admitted to conspiring to rob the bank and possessing offensive weapons.

Things were, however, more serious in Glasgow in December that same year, when a CID detective was shot dead and two others were wounded as police swooped during a hunt for bank raiders. It had been a desperate battle. The policeman fell under a hail of bullets as three men tried to fight their way from a tenement house in Glasgow. The officers had been alerted to look for the armed bandits who had stolen £35,000 in a daring bank raid at Linwood, Renfrewshire. An hour after the raid, policemen spotted three men hurrying from a car carrying suitcases. They followed the men to the doorway of a ground-floor flat in Allison Street, Govanhall, Glasgow. Fairy lights twinkled on a Christmas tree in the window. The police went into the living room of the flat, and immediately, shots rang out. DC Angus McKenzie, 32, fell dead at the feet of his colleagues, shot through the head. Another bullet struck DC Edward Barnett, 24, and a third wounded DI Andrew Hyslop in the neck. The other officer, DC John Campbell, disarmed one of the gunmen in a violent struggle. More policemen from a station 50yds along the street dashed to the scene, but one man, still armed, broke from the house. He got into a dark Ford Corsair with false number plates that was parked outside and sped away. Shortly afterwards, two men were taken in handcuffs from the house to the station nearby. DC Barnett was said to be gravely ill in hospital: a bullet was believed to be lodged in his brain, and he underwent emergency surgery. Hyslop was also very ill in hospital. McKenzie was married, and his wife, Jean, was informed of his death. Glasgow's chief constable, Sir James Robertson, said: "I am very deeply shocked. This is a very sad day for the Glasgow police and we are all deeply affected by the loss of our colleague and the attempts on the lives of two other colleagues."

Later that night, the two men were charged with murder and attempted murder. The third man was arrested afterwards by detectives in Paisley. He was also charged with murder and attempted murder, and all three appeared in Glasgow Sheriff's Court on 31st December. They were led in, handcuffed, less than 24 hours after the three officers had been shot. All three of the accused, Howard Wilson, John Sim and Ian Donaldson, faced charges of attempted murder and threatening to shoot another, as well as the murder of DC McKenzie. The men were remanded in custody as surgeons fought to save the lives of the two seriously injured officers. It was revealed that Barnett, married with two children, had been shot twice in the head and was "gravely ill"; Hyslop, 44, had been shot in the face and neck and was said to still be "seriously ill". The police fund launched in 1966 for police dependents received £12,000 from two businessmen following the shootings: Sir Hugh Fraser gave £7,000 from the Fraser Foundation and Sir Isaac Woolfson, Chairman of Great Universal Stores, gave £5,000.

On 4th January 1970, DC Edward Barnett died of his injuries in hospital. Barnett, who was only 25 years old, had remained unconscious since the shooting the previous Tuesday. The three men in custody were charged with the second murder. Police probed the £20,000 bank robbery, and started a hunt for another man who had mysteriously disappeared: this was revealed as the three men known to have been involved in the raid were sent for sentence in February 1970. Wilson, 31, had admitted the murder of both police officers, and also admitted, alongside Donaldson, 31, and Sim, 22, stealing more than £35,000 in two bank raids. Charges accusing former policeman Sim and mechanic Donaldson of the double murder were dropped by the prosecution. As the three were committed in custody to Edinburgh High Court, police announced that a warrant had been issued for the arrest of a fourth man in connection with the first robbery. They said that the man, who was unmarried, had vanished on Christmas Eve, five days before the second robbery. Earlier, the court was told that Donaldson, whose wife had a thalidomide baby, claimed to have sent two £400 packages of stolen money to the Thalidomide Appeal Fund. A spokesman at the Appeal Fund's London headquarters said later that they had not received any anonymous packages.

Ambition had grown in the mind of Howard Wilson like a disease. In just 18 months, it changed him from a good policeman into an uncontrollable killer. His dreams were well and truly brought to an end on 13th February 1970 when he was jailed for life for the murder of the two officers. Both belonged to the force of which for almost 10 years he had once been a respected member, being three times commended for initiative and devotion to duty. Wilson had proved himself an accomplished sportsman and a popular officer, but promotion was too slow for him, and ambition, for his wife and two baby sons as well as himself, led him to leave the police in July 1968 to improve his lot. With his police annuity he opened a fruit shop with another man, and it was successful at first. The men were persuaded against their better judgement to take on another shop, and as a result Wilson ran into debt. That was to lead him to plan and carry out his "perfect" first crime. This came off, so he was tempted by another – which went wrong, and ended in a frenzy of killing.

Cornered at his home, with the proceeds of a bank robbery, Wilson went berserk with a pistol. In minutes, one constable lay dead, another dying and a police inspector was badly wounded. His counsel told the court that Wilson had no sensible recollection of the shooting because he was numb with fear. He had been observed shouting meaningless expressions; he appeared to be completely out of control.

The details of Wilson's first crime were outlined by the Solicitor General for Scotland, Ewan Steward QC. Wilson and two other men, Sim and Donaldson, raided a bank stealing £13,000. But after paying off his debts, Wilson was left with nothing – and his debts piled up again. On 30th December 1969, the men raided another bank, getting away with £14,212. By chance a police car was passing by when Wilson and Donaldson were hurrying into the former policeman's house with suitcases. By chance one of the policemen, Hyslop, knew Wilson, and was pretty sure that he had embarked upon a life of crime since his time as an officer, suspecting that he was receiving whisky. When Wilson was asked about the suitcases he either invited in Hyslop and another officer named Sellers, or was happy to let them in. When Hyslop began to search the house and discovered the money, Wilson began to shoot. He pulled the trigger, but it jammed to start with, so he pulled back the sliding jacket of the weapon and cleared it. Hyslop rushed at Wilson but was shot down. The two other officers then entered the house, and both were shot down. Wilson deliberately stood over Barnett and shot him in the head. John Sellers took refuge in the bathroom. Wilson tried to open the door, but he was unable to take a shot at him. Wilson and Sim were eventually captured, but Donaldson made a run for it and was later caught. Menzies Campbell, defending Donaldson in court, said that the birth of the thalidomide child had greatly affected his character. In addition to life imprisonment, Wilson was jailed for 12 years for the two bank raids. The judge, Lord Grant, recommended that Wilson should serve at least 25 years. Sim and Donaldson were both jailed for 12 years for the bank raids.

1970 – Carry Out a Bank Raid, Then Live like a Country Squire

In February 1970, six armed men made off with £237,000 in a bank raid. The raiders, masked and dressed in black leather jackets, goggles and crash helmets, carried shotguns and a sledgehammer. The raid took only three minutes – in spite of a running battle as the bandits wrestled the money from the security guards. They had struck 20 minutes after the bank opened, and pushed through the doorway of Barclays Bank in Ilford, Essex, as three Security Express guards were banking the takings from a chain of East London supermarkets. They ordered the bank staff to lie face down on the floor behind the counter, then snatched six sealed money bags from the guards. As the men ran out, they knocked over a 72-year-old woman. She was taken to hospital with a broken finger and broken hip. Later, police found a Ford Transit van and a Ford Zephyr abandoned a mile away. Both vehicles had false number plates.

On 13th February, nine people, including four women, were charged with the raid. They had been detained after a series of swoops by detectives at addresses in North and East London, and appeared at Stratford magistrates' court the following day. Two days later, Securicor Express claimed £237,000 from Scotland Yard through its insurance company under the Riot Damages Act. It was suggested that the claim could be successful if lawyers proved a riot took place during the raid. The Yard considered the claim, but a Tory MP asked the Home Secretary, James Callaghan, if he had plans to amend the Act, which could see the police having to foot the bill in certain types of robberies. David Lane, MP for Cambridge, raised the query because a hotel in his constituency was planning on claiming £2,000 from Mid Anglia police under the Act, and he felt it was absurd that the police could be held financially responsible for damages and theft.

Three men who took part in the bank raid were jailed for a total of 51 years in November 1970. Two ringleaders, Ronald Dark, 36, and Michael Green, 29, were each jailed for 18 years. A third man, Arthur Saunders, 33, was given 15 years. An Old Bailey jury found them guilty of conspiring to rob and of taking part in the robbery. The well-laid plans came unstuck when detectives interviewed a Security Express guard, 54-year-old Edward McCarthy, who confessed to being one of the intelligence agents from whom Dark and Green had got information needed to plan the raid. He was jailed for six years after admitting conspiracy to rob. Two other men also pleaded guilty to a similar charge: Charles Bowman, 27, and Albert Walker, 44, received three years and four years respectively.

Dark, who had twice escaped from prison, was caught five months after the raid living in a remote farm near Lapford in Devon. He was known locally as a wealthy country type who went hunting on his own horses. At the end of January 1971, a court heard how his mistress lived with him in the lap of luxury. Barbara Hepburn, 28, pleaded not guilty to handling stolen goods between February and April 1970; she also denied conspiracy to help Dark to escape arrest between October 1968 and July 1970. The two men who appeared with her were William Love, 45, and Alfred Prill, 36, who also pleaded not guilty to helping Dark escape arrest. Hepburn was found guilty of living off the proceeds of the bank raid in Ilford by an Old Bailey jury, and of conspiring to obstruct the course of public justice. She was jailed for two years, but only served nine months and was freed on 12th November 1971. Three Appeal Court judges decided that she did not play a leading part in helping Dark, even though she lived with him in Lapford, posing as his wife.

On 21st October 1970 a bank raider lost a haul by losing his cool and bungling the job from start to finish. It was 11.15am when a man walked into a tiny Lloyds Bank sub-branch in Banstead, Surrey. He tried to look calm, but soon showed he wasn't. When he pointed a pistol at 21-year-old cashier, Colin Wade, and demanded money, Colin bravely reached under the counter screen and tried to grab the gun. Instead of running off, the gunman fired, and Colin collapsed with a stomach wound. Having fired, the gunman left the bank and started sprinting towards Banstead railway station. Still clutching his gun, he dashed through a nearby block of flats, but tripped on a step outside the flat of Florrie Martin, 62. His pistol went flying, and a frightened Mrs Martin found it at her feet. The gunman picked up the gun and ran off, and a few minutes later the police arrived. They thought the man had got on a London-bound train and later stopped a train and searched it, but they didn't find the man, who was said to be in his 20s. It was Florrie Martin who called the police: she had seen the man acting suspiciously before the raid, and called them before he even walked into the bank. Wade was said to be in a satisfactory condition in hospital, but needed an operation to remove the bullet from his stomach.

A security guard in the City of London was not so lucky. On 1st December 1970, Raymond Harden from Essex a 38-year-old married man with two children, was coshed by an armed raider. The bandits had entered the National Westminster Bank on Cornhill while a Securicor van was parked outside. The guards had loaded seven cash boxes onto a trolley just inside the door of the building when four men rushed in. One had a shotgun, two had coshes and the fourth had a pistol. Mr Harden, who had crossed the pavement to get another box from the van, was felled to the ground by a vicious blow on the back of his head with a heavy iron bar. Two bank messengers who tackled the raiders were injured: one was coshed, the other was shot. Within two minutes, the gang had grabbed the seven boxes and fled. They ran past the guard, who was dying in his own blood, along Cornhill, then left into St Michael's Alley. Two civilians tried to tackle them, and both were coshed. In George Yard, a van was waiting for the men. It drove to Lombard Street, then disappeared: it was found later in a multi-storey car park less than a mile away. The money boxes had gone, together with about £2,000 in silver, but two valuable clues had been left behind: a pair of light-brown tortoiseshell glasses and a red/brown Gladstone-type bag. Police believed that the raiders had worn false moustaches: one of them had been seen shortly before the raid, and the wind had been blowing his moustache away from his face. Raymond

Harden died in hospital, and police immediately launched a major murder investigation. Four men went to Wood Lane police station following the incident, where they agreed to help with inquiries. Five men were wanted in connection with the innocent man's death and the raid, and the *Mirror*'s Crime Bureau gave careful descriptions of each of them on 22nd December: the newspaper described them as the five most wanted men in Britain after they continued to evade police. Many people volunteered information, which had helped, but police needed to close the net still further.

That same month, PC "Big John" Pitcher saved a baby from armed gun raiders when he defied them while armed only with a truncheon. As five bandits grabbed a £70,000 haul, two others stood guard outside the bank doorway. PC Pitcher, who had heard the bank alarm, saw them as he ran towards the bank with his truncheon in his hand. He stopped, and pushed women and children who were watching around a corner. Then he saw a baby in a pushchair under a shotgun that was being held by one of the bandits. He went up to the robber, pointed at the baby, and when the gunman nodded, he picked up the pushchair and baby and carried the child to safety. When he returned, the bandits were driving off from the Midland Bank in North London.

"I didn't tackle the raiders because, when you are confronted with half-a-dozen blokes armed with sawn-off shotguns, and you only have a thick stick of wood, you don't do anything unless you want to go to an early grave," said Pitcher. The bandits had already shot one man. He added: "I didn't want to be blown to pieces. I have a wife and kid to think of ... For £20 a week, when you're only armed with a truncheon, what can you do?" The raid started when the gang – wearing balaclava helmets and stocking masks – blocked the street outside the bank with a van. Five of them rushed into the bank, where they shot a 19-year-old customer in the hand, coshed another customer and squirted ammonia in the face of a third. The youth who was shot lost the tips of some of his fingers. Three of the raiders leapt over the counter's protective screen and scooped up the money, then carried the bags in a human chain to a blue van, in which they escaped.

Also in December 1970, a bank robber stopped in the middle of his hold-up to give radio listeners a live running commentary. Radio news reported that the presenter Don Harris phoned a bank in Chicago after hearing about the hold-up. "I understand you've got a robbery there," said Harris to the man who answered the phone. "Yes," said the man. "This is the robber speaking." "What are you doing in there?" asked Harris, as his audience listened. "Well I just want to tell you honestly that I tried to make it the shortest possible way and it's the wrong way," said the bandit. He then told the radio audience that he was surrounded, and would just like a moment because he was going to take his own life. There was a clatter as he dropped the phone, and then the police could be heard moving in on him and demanding he hand over his gun. They arrested Anthony Yockley, 27. Radio listeners had thought the call was either a hoax or a comedy show: they just couldn't believe that a raider would answer the phone while in the middle of a hold-up.

1971 – Night Chase, Kidnap and a Police Probe for the Raid that Shouldn't Have Been

Armed police were out early on 25th March 1971, hunting a gang of seven bank robbers who gunned down a policeman. The gangsters hijacked two cars, and forced a motorist to drive at gunpoint in a bid to escape a huge police dragnet. Later, an 80mph car chase ended in a smash in which five men were injured and taken to hospital. The gang, armed with sawn-off shotguns and a pistol, pounced as an armoured security van was delivering money to the NatWest Bank in Gravesend. They grabbed £30,000, hurled it into a white Ford Escort van, then piled in and drove off. Fourteen miles away, at Knockholt, PC Peter Dinsdale, 23, was patrolling in his panda car when he saw the bandits' van. He knew nothing of the bank raid, but was suspicious of the heavily laden van and followed it.

The bandits cut in front of his car, forcing him to stop. Then, as PC Dinsdale put out a radio call for help, one of the bandits squirted ammonia in his face. Blinded, he was dragged out of his car and hurled to the ground. Two shots were fired, and the PC was hit in the leg by a .22 bullet. He managed to stagger to a nearby house and phoned for help. Despite his injuries, he helped his colleagues to search for the van, and they found it abandoned about a mile away. He was taken to hospital for an operation to remove the bullet, but his condition was not said to be serious. While the search for the seven men continued, a motorist reported that his van had been hijacked by five gunmen between Knockholt and Westerham. The van was later found in Tatsfield, Surrey: in it were some bags of coins. Later, another motorist told police at Westerham that his car had been commandeered by gunmen at Tatsfield. They held a pistol to his head and forced him to drive to Woldingham railway station. The gangsters ordered Anthony Fairrle to keep his head down while they escaped. As the search went on, police were told that yet another car had been stolen from outside the railway station. The green Cortina was spotted by police on Thanet Way outside Ramsgate with five men in it. The driver ignored police warnings to stop, and was chased at speeds of up to 80mph. Then, at a crossroads near Pegwell Bay, the green car crashed. The men were taken to Thanet accident unit, where it was later reported that three had serious injuries. Two other men, not in the car at the time of the crash, were still being hunted by Surrey, Kent and London police.

In another story, from September 1971, a bank official was forced to open his bank's vaults at gunpoint after a night of terror in which he and his wife were held captive in their own home. The gang got away with £90,000 from the bank in Sunbury, Surrey, leaving the entire staff locked up in the vaults. The drama began when three masked men burst into the home of assistant manager Norman Horne and his wife Marion in Long Ditton. The men jumped through the front door of the couple's home as Marion opened the door to take the dog for a walk.

Mrs Horne was coshed, and the couple were told that they would be safe as long as they did as they were told and didn't move about too much. If they did not comply then they would be shot. At 6.30am the following day, the couple were driven blindfolded in a van to the bank. Norman was forced to open the main safe while one of the gang held a gun to his wife's head. Then the raiders, armed with pistols and a sawn-off shotgun, grabbed the staff as they arrived and locked them in a broom cupboard. When the gang had finished, all the staff were herded into the vaults and locked in. Forty-five minutes later, help arrived: police forced a back door after customers found the bank closed. Mrs Horne was taken to hospital to have stitches put in her head wound. One of the imprisoned staff was manager Guy Whitmarsh, who was met by a man with a sawn-off shotgun as he arrived for work. He tried to get a look at the raiders, but his head was turned away.

In September 1971, detectives listened in as a gang stripped the strongroom of a bank in London. There was a big question mark over their handling of the situation, though, and Scotland Yard tried to find out just how the bandits beat the tremendous odds stacked against them to escape with a huge haul. During a weekend grab of money and jewels from the Lloyds Bank at the junction of Baker Street and Marylebone Road, the raiders had dodged the bank's security system by tunnelling into the vault from a shop two doors away, and bursting into the bank with a thermic lance. Using walkie-talkie radios to keep in touch with a look-out man posted at the top of a block of flats, they had managed to foil London's police. Officers were tipped off about the robbery by a radio amateur, who picked up the walkie-talkie signals.

The gang – including a woman – had a huge stroke of luck, as police set about checking 700 London banks following the alert. They were cracking safe-deposit boxes in the vault when Lloyds security inspectors and police officers arrived on the scene. The raiders kept quiet and sat tight, as bank staff and police determined that alarms were in order and the vault doors had not been tampered with. The investigating team left, assuming that everything was all right, and the raiders continued opening safe-deposit boxes, some of which contained valuables worth up to £500,000. They escaped with their haul on the Sunday afternoon.

Scotland Yard wanted to know why the Post Office detector service was not called until midday on the Sunday, when it was too late for them to do anything. The gang had toiled for 13 hours tunnelling into the bank's vault, and for most of that time, police were listening to the two-way radio conversation between the raiders and their look-out man. Radio amateur Robert Rowlands, 32, picked up the gang's signals over the radio just as he was going to bed at his flat in Wimpole Street about half a mile away from the bank, at around 11.30pm. He began recording the conversations he was hearing when he heard one of the men say: "We're sitting on £500,000." He then alerted police. One of the voices was believed to be that of a gang member posted on the top of a block of flats with a pair of binoculars. Police thought he was stationed there to watch for anyone who might be showing a dangerous interest in the bank. Some of the conversation follows:

First raider: "Listen carefully. We want you to mind for one hour from now until approximately one o'clock and then to go off the air, get some sleep and come on the air with both radios at six o'clock in the morning."

Second raider: "This is not a very good pitch during the day. You know that, don't you? It's all blowing about and everything."

First raider: "Are you sure you will be on the street tomorrow? I suggest we carry on tonight, mate, and get it done with. Look, the place is filled with fumes where we was cutting. And if the security come in and smell the fumes we are all going to get stopped and none of us have got nothing. This way, we have all got 300 grand to cut up when we come back in the morning."

The man on the roof did not appear to be very happy with the arrangement, and told his fellow gang member that he wasn't going to be any good the following day. He was advised by the first raider to get some sleep, but the pleading from the roof continued. The night seemed to pass uneventfully for the look-out, who reported in the morning that everything was fine.

During the hunt for the robbers, police checked on the bank, but like the security staff they could find nothing amiss. Their crucial mistake, however, was not opening the doors to the vault. The raid was discovered on Monday 13th September by bank manager Guy Darke, long after the gang had gone. It was determined that the gang had tunnelled more than 40ft through sand and earth from the handbag shop two doors away before they reached the 4ft-thick reinforced concrete floor of the bank vault. Post Office engineers failed to get an accurate fix on the locations of the walkie-talkies, and the police search ended in failure. The gang had left behind their tools, including the radio set, hammers, picks, shovels, gas cylinders and thermic lances. Police also found half-eaten food and flasks, and most of the basement of the neighbouring shop was full of earth that had come from the tunnel.

Security guards at Lloyds were stunned by the news that an "impregnable" vault had been broken into. A bank spokesman said: "Our security people who went with the police to the bank were satisfied that everything was working properly on Sunday, and that nothing had been tampered with. Our security system is comprehensive and very complicated. It appeared to the inspection team that there was absolutely nothing wrong."

Police were puzzled by the small size of the hole through which the raiders got into the vault. It was only 15in wide, so police suspected that a small woman or a child might have been involved; one of the voices picked up on the radio was a woman. Senior detectives agreed that the job was brilliantly professional, but wondered if the gang had been disturbed, as only a quarter of the safe-deposit boxes were robbed. Guy Darke was stunned by the news that his bank had been raided. Returning from holiday, he was overwhelmed with safe-deposit box holders demanding news of their valuables, despite the fact that the bank was closed for

Monday following the robbery. "One couple, told
...eir valuables worth £5,000 were safe, kept hugging each
other with tears pouring down their faces," said the bank manager.

Just two days after the robbery, an inquiry into the way police handled the bank raid was started by Scotland Yard. The investigating team were told to find out whether the police were negligent as the thieves tunnelled their way into the vault. Despite police listening into the live walkie-talkie conversations, they failed to ask engineers to trace the source of the radios until 12½ hours after the raid began. By then it was too late: the signals had stopped. The case became more mysterious when former washing machine tycoon John Bloom denied having a safe-deposit box at the bank with valuables worth up to £100,000. It was reported to be one of the 215 smashed boxes robbed during the raid, but Bloom was adamant the box wasn't his. His wife confirmed that the couple had used the branch in 1966, but stated categorically that they had never had an account at the bank. However, someone called John Bloom lost around £70,000-worth of gems and £30,000 of cash in the raid. The most valuable loss was thought to be a sheaf of confidential papers containing the names of businesspeople and details of planned business ventures, including details of plans to sell colour televisions for £72.

Meanwhile, police concentrated their efforts on a country mansion, thought to be the home of the man who had plotted and financed the robbery. By the end of the month during which the raid took place, the value of the booty was estimated to be around

£4m, as detectives slowly traced the owners of 50 of the 215 safe-deposit boxes which were smashed open. The estimated total made the robbery the largest ever heist in Britain at the time – bigger than the Great Train Robbery some eight years before, with a total of £2.6m – even though very little of the haul appeared to be in cash: for the most part, it was gold, diamonds and other gems. By 24th September, detectives had the names of two men that they wanted to interview, both of whom were well known in London circles; both had also disappeared from their usual haunts. One was said to be a dead ringer for the film star Kirk Douglas, with a prominent cleft chin, while police were also hunting for a mysterious woman, who had been spotted on several occasions shopping in the area before the robbery. A number of witnesses had described the woman, who wore a variety of wigs.

Police had found three of the raiders by January 1973: they admitted entering the bank, stealing cash and valuables and possessing explosives. Thomas Stevens, 33, from Islington, Reginald Tucker, 37, of Lee Street, Hackney, and 38-year-old Anthony Gavin from Dalston were on trial at the Old Bailey. However, Benjamin Wolfe, 64, from East Dulwich, denied charges, while uncle and nephew, Abdullah Gangji, 62, and Ackbar Gangji, 22, denied receiving £32,000 in stolen notes and helping to dispose of the money. The raid, which played out just around the corner from Sherlock Holmes' fictional address on Baker Street, was dubbed "The Baker Street Moles". In fact it was almost a carbon copy of one of the most famous robberies in fiction. *The*

Red-Headed League is a short story by Sir Arthur Conan Doyle, written in 1890,which follows the story of a group of criminals who take over a pawnbroker's shop adjoining a London bank before attempting a robbery. The thieves patiently tunnelled for days between shop and bank before being caught by Sherlock Holmes. It took Scotland Yard slightly longer than the fictional detective to bring the perpetrators to justice.

By now, the final amount stolen had been confirmed at £3m; it was Britain's biggest robbery to date. Despite the fact that four men were in custody over the raid, only £231,000 had been recovered. Facing the jury at the Old Bailey was Tucker, convicted and sentenced to 12 years for his part in the robbery. The former funfair attendant, newsagent and car dealer was recruited as the gang's reconnaissance man. He had opened a safe-deposit account at the bank (although he had little to deposit) so that he could gain access to the bank's vaults and make copies of their layout. While in the vaults alone, Tucker showed ingenuity by measuring the room using his umbrella. His share of the loot was left in a luggage locker at Waterloo station. Stephens, a car dealer, was also jailed for 12 years. He had provided the tools for digging the tunnel and had helped by removing 15 tons of rubble. The man who planned and constructed the tunnel was Gavin, who also received a 12-year sentence. Gavin had lost 1½ stone while carrying out the preliminary digging towards the bank vault from the neighbouring handbag shop. His loot was left in a locker at Euston station. Benjamin Wolfe was jailed for eight years for his part in the heist, as the judge,

Edward Sutcliffe QC, did not wa[...]
of his life in prison. The leather [...]
been taken over by Wolfe, who d[...]
the gang breaking into the bank. [...]
authorities were mindful that the [...]
was nowhere near the court and [...]
the gang. Derek Larkins was want[...]
was a man known as Ginger John [...]
by Gavin).

that the bank had been p[...]

raid. Before the raid [...]

14 occasions, [...]

when allo[...]

piled [...]

At a special press conference at Scotland Yard, CID Commander Robert Huntley defended the way that the bank robbery was investigated, saying that three West London police divisions were alerted to the raid but had no way of pinpointing the bank inside a wide radius. Radio amateur Rowlands had picked up the sound of roadworks and other clues, but there were six other banks and four other buildings holding large amounts of cash in the area that could have been involved. Commander Huntley revealed that detectives twice asked the Post Office for detector vans to track down the bandits' radios, but no help was forthcoming. He also pointed out that the press had been asked not to print the contents of the conversations picked up by Rowlands, yet they had, and he claimed that this had led to a lengthened police investigation. In addition, the police were prohibited by Lloyds Bank for quite some time from knowing who the victims were and what had been taken.

In 1977, the High Court in London was told by Raymond Kidwell QC that the security at Lloyds Bank was "wholly inefficient" and

...egligent both before and after the 1971 ..., gang member Tucker had cased the joint on ...while after the raid the bank was less than vigilant ...wing people in to take their valuables, which were left ...on tables. In some cases, people weren't even checked to see if they were depositors. Kidwell argued in court that: "The system would have facilitated and doubtless did facilitate, people getting valuables which were not theirs. Property went widely and wildly astray." The QC was representing 139 people claiming £666,000 in valuables stolen in the robbery. The bank claimed that it was not responsible for the losses unless negligence could be proved.

1973 – Laurel and Hardy in Slapstick Bank Raid

While bank raids are a heinous crime and can end in fatalities, they do have a more amusing side when hapless criminals get in on the act. In Italy in January 1973, two raiders who acted like Laurel and Hardy went through a laugh-a-minute routine before an audience of one customer and seven bank clerks. Things started to go wrong for the masked robbers before they even got into the bank in Milan. When they strode from their car up to the bank's glass doors one of them walked smack into a fixed pane and nearly knocked himself out. Once inside, the bandit with a bump on his head indicated his pistol-packing partner and announced: "This is a hold-up." Then, just as if he was in a movie, he tried to vault over the counter. Being less agile than he had thought, he landed on a typewriter, smashing it to bits. Undaunted, he began to scoop money out of the cash desk, watched by the bemused staff and customer. He missed the drawer containing bundles of 50,000 lire and 100,000 lire notes and tried to stuff his pockets full of 10,000 lire notes (worth about £7 each). His overcoat turned out not to have any pockets, so he stuffed the cash into a typewriter cover. When he vaulted back over the counter with his loot, he crashed to the floor and spilt all the money. His accomplice's patience was exhausted, and he snapped: "Pull yourself together, or I'll shoot you!" The pair fled with a haul of about £3,000, leaving a trail of scattered banknotes.

It was a little more serious back in Britain the following month, when a housewife saved her local bobby from a gunman during a bank raid. One of the five raiders pointed a shotgun at PC Graham McClarty, but the 39-year-old woman ran towards the gunman and shouted: "Don't you shoot our policeman." The gunman, unnerved by the shouting, hesitated and fled with the gang, who escaped with £4,000. Police commended the woman for her bravery, but she asked for her identity to be kept secret because she didn't want any fuss. The woman had just taken her two children to school when the masked raiders attacked a Securicor van outside a bank in Lambeth. The gang grabbed a bag of money, which was being delivered to the bank, and fired the shotgun as a warning; they ran from the van as the policeman appeared, while the man with the shotgun held up the policeman as the other four raiders made their getaway. McClarty, who was married with a two-year-old son, said: "I was on traffic duty and heard what sounded like a shot coming from the bank. I ran up the road, the gunman levelled the gun at me and shouted: 'Get down and keep down.' I turned away expecting a shot. Seconds later I looked up and saw the man running away. I understand the woman shouted at the man as he was about to fire."

1975 – £2m Stolen from Bank of America

When news was announced of a Bank of America robbery in April 1975, it was estimated that bandits had got away with a staggering £2m. And, it looked as if it wasn't the gang's first attempt at an American bank. In November 1974, robbers were foiled because their drills were too short to penetrate the massive vault door fully. Dubbed the Mayfair Mob, they made no such mistake when four armed raiders drilled their way into the vault at the Davies Street branch of the Bank of America. They used a jemmy to force open 89 safe-deposit boxes and got away with £250,000 in cash – they ignored £1m in travellers' cheques, which would have been hard to get rid off – and an extremely valuable haul of gems and other valuables. At this time, the California-based Bank of America was the world's largest bank, and the robbery was cited as one of the biggest hauls in recent years.

One customer, Farida Hall, 38, put her uninsured loss at £200,000, which was her entire jewellery collection, including nine rings, two diamond brooches, two diamond pendants and five pairs of jewelled earrings. Mrs Hall, the daughter of a sugar exporter, had kept her jewellery in the bank for eight years, and had never insured her property as she believed it to be safe in the bank. Police and bank officials contacted all keyholders whose boxes were rifled, but the major headache for the investigation was to establish what had been taken from the confidential boxes. One depositor,

American businessman John Pugliese, had six gold coins worth up to six figures in his deposit box; he was, however, insured. One particularly worried customer was 23-year-old student John Phillips, from Bloomsbury, who had a number of gold coins worth several thousand pounds.

The raid was discovered by a patrolling security guard who reached the bank at 8.38pm and found three staff – two men and a woman – bound and gagged. They had been working late in an upstairs office when they were caught by the gang. One of the gang had hidden inside the bank until it closed in order to let other members inside; this was the same method used by the gang in November the previous year. The man hiding inside the bank knocked out the alarm system and kicked in the door to an underground passage in Three Kings Yard before unlocking the door and allowing his fellow accomplices into the premises. The plan – despite the three late workers – went like clockwork, and in the words of one senior detective was the work of "a good team of professional thieves".

The gang had detailed knowledge of the bank's layout, and the alarms were shut down easily and quickly. After they tied up the members of staff in the basement, they made their way into the vault using drills. All four gang members were armed, and seemed to possess information about the structure of the combination lock on the steel vault door. Using an ordinary power drill, they bored through points on the lock near the combination numbers. Once inside, they loaded their haul into bags, then left the bank through the underground passage. Just eight minutes later – and two hours after the robbery began – Bob Gordon discovered the crime on his rounds.

Police investigations led them to 32-year-old James O'Loughlin, who was tried at London's Marlborough Street magistrates' court on 28th July 1975. He was accused of conspiracy in the raid, and police watched in puzzlement as O'Loughlin, from Gate Road, Kingston, Surrey, made bail. He walked calmly by them and left the court, and it became clear that the criminal, who stood charged alongside five other men, had asked to go to the toilet in order to calmly make his escape. The men had been remanded in custody until August, and had left the dock to make their way to the cells below to await a prison van. O'Loughlin left the toilet and walked past other prisoners, tricking court police into thinking that he had been granted bail. A hurried search around the court once the alarm was raised confirmed that he had managed to make a break for freedom.

At the end of September 1975, electronics expert Stuart Buckley was jailed for seven years at the Old Bailey when the court heard how he had used an ingenious method to find the combination of the bank safe. He had watched through a spyhole in a false ceiling when he was working as an electrical contractor, and seen the manager operate the dial. He then tipped off the gang. Buckley admitted to stealing £2¼m from the Bank of America, but became a marked man for naming the rest of the gang. Buckley had been given a job with the bank as an electrician just nine months after being released from prison. Bank of America never knew he was a crook and he soon became trusted by other staff members. He was given access to all the bank's branches in London, and was able to gain most of the keys to all areas.

By March 1976, police believed that the gang had got away with £8m, as owners of 85 of the deposit boxes had revealed how much they had lost in cash and valuables. By this time, there were 17 people awaiting trial in connection with the crime. On 11th June that same year, company director John O'Connell, 41, was gunned down as he made his way from his home to a bus stop nearby to face trial. The hitman was hiding behind a bush in a churchyard, and was believed to have escaped in a car, probably driven by an accomplice, after he blasted O'Connell with a shotgun. O'Connell had been struck in the leg, and was rushed to hospital from Church Vale, East Finchley, for an emergency operation. He had been due to appear at the Old Bailey alongside seven other men and a woman. Key witnesses had been given armed bodyguards for some time, and following this attack the judge, Alan King-Hamilton, said that jury members would be given a police escort to and from the court.

In November 1976, three men were found guilty of the robbery: Leonard Wilde, 51, Peter Colson, 32, and William Gear, 44. Wilde's wife, Vivienne, 41, was found not guilty of receiving. But later in November, five men received jail sentences for a total of more than 100 years. White – an underworld locksmith – was given the longest sentence at 23 years. He was also sentenced to 12 years for the earlier plot to rob the bank in November 1974, which was to run concurrently. Colson was jailed for 21 years, Gear got 18 years, O'Loughlin – who had been recaptured – got 17 years, and the fifth man, 52-year-old Henry Jeffery received 12 years. Henry Taylor, a greengrocer who let the robbers use his shop to share out the loot, was given three years. Croupier Edward Gerty, 34, received two years for receiving stolen money and jewellery, and Michael Gervaise, 33, found guilty of taking part in the first unsuccessful plan, was jailed for 18 months. As the star prosecution witness, Buckley was said to be in fear of his life. The missing treasure, however, had not been found.

The man the papers called "Mr Big", ringleader Frank Maple, 37, had escaped to his villa in Marbella, Spain, following the first raid in 1974. Following a big round-up by Scotland Yard, he was arrested, and then released because extradition papers did not arrive from London in time. Maple then fled to Morocco, which had no extradition treaty with Britain. He was known to have been involved in other London heists, including defrauding Christie's and Sotheby's auction rooms. Maple's mistake was to move country. He was arrested in Greece in June 1977, and police believed that he would be extradited to Britain. However, the former gang leader was also wanted in Austria in connection with the theft of £120,000 in cash and jewellery in an armed raid at a ski resort in February that year. As the tug of war for custody of Maple raged on, Scotland Yard announced that they also wanted 35-year-old David Carroll, known as Boy-Boy, who had vanished after the

Mayfair raid. Eventually, in September 1977, Austria won the fight to extradite Maple. Meanwhile, O'Connell, who had been crippled by an unknown hitman, hobbled to freedom from the Old Bailey in December having been given a two-year suspended sentence, 12 months after other members of the gang were jailed.

Frank Maple was jailed for nine years in April 1978 for the Austrian robbery. He was due to be extradited to Britain once he had served a third of his sentence. The following year, Viv Wilde went into hiding after claiming that a high-ranking police officer was paid more than £7,000 for acting as "Mr Fix-it" for the gang. Police feared that a contract had been put out on Mrs Wilde's life for grassing on the officer, and for claiming that he was paid money for the deals he made with criminals to protect them from prosecution. Police had mounted Operation Countryman, which was ongoing at the time, to look into the allegations, and five officers had already been suspended. Then on 5th November 1982, Frank Maple walked free from the Old Bailey after the prosecution offered no evidence against him. Peter Colson didn't learn that crime doesn't pay, as he was caught trying to rob a security van in November 1987 while posing as a dispatch rider. He had only been free for a year, having served his sentence for the Bank of America crime. He received a new sentence of 16 years.

1976 – Bank Raid Bungled by One-Eyed Bandit

A one-eyed bandit made a glaring error when he set out on a bank raid: he wore a hood over his head with only one eyehole in it. The bandit, 25-year-old Alan Wells, didn't bother to cut a second hole for his blind eye. His Nelson-type mask gave police the vital clue they needed in their hunt for him. After a 31-day trial at the Old Bailey, the careless crook received a 14-year jail sentence.

Wells, from Brentford, Essex, was found guilty of taking part in two robberies and plotting another two. A second man, Leslie Joyce, 23, from Hornchurch, also in Essex, got 14 years on the same charges. The jury took four days and three nights to consider their verdict. The slip-up over the mask came when Wells and Joyce raided a bank in Manchester in October 1974. They helped themselves to cash without realizing that the one-eyed mask was very obvious to the bank staff. Four of the six other men accused with Wells and Joyce were convicted of conspiring to rob. They were Frank Wilson, 34, Michael McGrath, 26, Michael Delorie, 25, and Geoffrey Cunliffe, 23.

It was also in 1976 that the unholy clergyman Stephen Care decided to rob the church where he preached each Sunday. Pinching pennies from the Sunday School collection came as easily to Care as conning insurance firms out of hundreds of pounds.

The most astonishing moment in the greedy clergyman's crime spree came when he took his frail old housekeeper on a bank raid. The "Biddy and Clyde" pair, as newspapers dubbed them, netted £1,775, and calmly made their getaway in a taxi. The 32-year-old parson was caught on 26th February, and he was sentenced to seven years imprisonment. A jury at Exeter Crown Court heard that he used his dog collar to gain trust in a criminal career that saw him steal £19,029. It was the clerical collar and all that went with it that first attracted Care to the Church when he was a schoolboy in the Cornish village of St Ives. He didn't have a strong religious vocation, but he adored the idea of dressing up. The fact that he wasn't bright didn't deter him either. Delusions of grandeur were only the start for Care, who lived in a Walter Mitty world of fantasy. He loved expensive restaurants and high living, but this all came at a price. Many of his bills were picked up by others, including families whose homes in Paignton were raided by the curate and three parsons who had their vicarages burgled. Much of the money that parishioners gave ended up in his pocket. The sticky-fingered clergyman, who robbed just about anybody and everybody, travelled to Penzance to sell a silver kettle he had swiped from a school. The kettle later changed hands – twice – and ended up in an antique shop in Torquay. It was back, almost on Care's doorstep. By sheer chance it was spotted in the shop window by Dorothy O'Brien, who ran Greylands School from where it had been stolen. Detectives traced the kettle back to Care, and suddenly it was realized that the police had solved a crime wave. When police went to his new vicarage in Plymouth, they found an Aladdin's cave of stolen property.

Hardened detectives were stunned by the Biddy and Clyde bank robbery, though. The two unlikely raiders broke just about every rule in the criminal book, yet they managed a clean getaway. Clyde was Care, who masterminded the audacious raid on Lloyds Bank in Plymouth. Biddy was his frail and deaf housekeeper, Stella Bunting, 58. When Care outlined his plan to Bunting at the vicarage in Paignton, the woman was far from keen; but Care was persuasive, and convinced the simple-minded woman that they would be like Robin Hood stealing from the rich to give to the poor. The housekeeper agreed to take part in the raid, and they left for the bank by taxi.

Care wore the most ridiculous of disguises – a flat cap, a false moustache and a piece of plaster over his nose. When he got into the bank manager's office he announced that he had planted a bomb in the building and could trigger it by a transmitter in his pocket. Cash was duly handed over, and the couple retreated to their waiting taxi. The bank raid was the most spectacular escapade in Care's two-year crime spree. It had begun with an easy £700 payout from an insurance company after he claimed his vicarage had been robbed; then he raided five homes, and picked up antiques and other items worth more than £1,500. His biggest haul came when he snatched £12,000-worth of gem-studded vestments from Buckfast Abbey. This was followed by the bank raid. Just before he was arrested, Care snaffled £72 from the funds of his new church – St Chad's in Whitleigh, Plymouth.

By the latter decades of the 20th century, bank raids had become few and far between. It seemed that the days of "smash and grab" at gunpoint were over, with criminals targeting other areas of financial distribution. Banks had wised up to securing their buildings, and the criminals who had enjoyed "rear-entry" break-ins found that their routes were barred, as security at the back and the sides of banks became just as extensive as at the front. In addition, computer technology and other technologies meant that robbing banks had become virtually a thing of the past. In the 1990s, it was much more likely that as the end of the decade gave way to the new millennium, elaborate schemes to rob would include frauds and swindles – especially within companies. Banks did have another force to be reckoned with, however – cybercrime.